HOW TO DISCOVER
YOUR SPIRITUAL GIFTS

Lay Action Ministry Program
5827 S. Rapp St.
Littleton, CO 80120

David C. Cook Publishing Co.
850 N. Grove Ave.
Elgin, IL 60120

Scripture quotations, unless otherwise noted, are taken from the Holy Bible: New International Version, © 1973, 1978, 1984 by the International Bible Society, used by permission of Zondervan Bible Publishers.

Quotes from *Unwrap Your Spiritual Gifts* by Kenneth Gangel, and from *19 Gifts of the Spirit* by Leslie B. Flynn are used by permission of Victor Books, P.O. Box 1825, Wheaton, IL 60189.

David C. Cook Publishing Co.
850 North Grove Avenue
Elgin, IL 60120
Printed in U.S.A

Editor: Gary Wilde
Designer: Chris Patchel
Cover: Lois Rosio Sprague

ISBN: 1-55513-016-X
Library of Congress Catalog Number: 87-72831

TABLE OF
CONTENTS

LAY ACTION
MINISTRY PROGRAM

LAMP courses are based on the HEAD, HEART, and HANDS approach to learning. HEAD represents Bible *content* that you want to know. HEART represents your *personal application* of the truth. HANDS refers to the LAMP goal of preparing you to *use content in the lives of other people*—imparting to others what you have learned (see II Tim. 2:2).

The believer in Christ has been lavished with the riches of God's grace (Eph. 1:7, 8) and the spiritual gifts required for effective ministry to others. But in the lives of many Christians this spiritual wealth remains buried treasure. Though searching for lost treasure is a challenging occupation, those who persevere with single-minded persistence can find themselves fabulously wealthy. *How to Discover Your Spiritual Gifts* can lead you into a whole new way of seeing your value as a ministering member of Christ's Body, the Church.

Course Objectives
- Arrive at a basic understanding of what the New Testament teaches on the subject of spiritual gifts.
- Begin the journey of personal spiritual gift discovery and use.
- Develop a desire to be used of God in ministry to God and others.

Course Requirements

This course is for every Christian who is willing to put forth the effort in personal study. But we want you to know "up front" what it is going to cost you in terms of time and commitment. First, *it is going to cost you a good hour of home study for each lesson.* Make every effort to spend this much time as a minimum requirement.

How to Use This Course

Though you may complete the course by yourself, you will normally be preparing for a weekly group meeting. In this meeting you will be an active participant because of your personal study. One lesson is to be completed each week, prior to coming to the weekly group meeting.

The group meeting features a discussion of the lesson that you have studied during the week. It also includes other elements to encourage group life, and to guide group members toward personal application of the material. The meeting, planned for at least a full hour, should be led by a person who enjoys leading discussions and helping people learn. The study leader will study the lesson in the same way as anyone else in the group, with the aid of the four-step lesson plans at the back of the book. In addition, a fuller, more detailed Leader's Guide can be obtained from:

DAVID C. COOK PUBLISHING CO.
850 NORTH GROVE AVENUE
ELGIN, IL 60120
or:
LAY ACTION MINISTRY PROGRAM, INC.
5827 S. RAPP STREET
LITTLETON, CO 80120

1

YOU ARE THE BODY OF CHRIST

The whole subject of spiritual gifts is the lost treasure of the 19th and 20th century Christianity. The Church has been impoverished beyond belief by the prevailing ignorance of the existence of these spiritual riches. But now the long-buried truth is coming to light again. Widespread excitement has possessed the churches, and the tide of interest in the subject is running at full flow.
—Ray Stedman, quoted in Kenneth Gangel, *Unwrap Your Spiritual Gifts*

We're going to go look for that lost treasure! Using careful and profitable "mining" techniques, we'll start finding the pure gold of God's riches in the area of spiritual gifts. Let's begin digging in the mother lode of the Scriptures—God's Word.

The Continuing Ministry of Jesus Christ

Spiritual life is the direct continuing ministry of Jesus Christ in the believer. And the Holy Spirit is the source of this "Christlife." Thus, spiritual gifts are directly related to spiritual life.

Begin by asking yourself, "What was the ministry of Jesus Christ?" and "How does that relate to the Christian's *present* ministry?" Answer this two-fold question from the following passages in the Book of Mark.

Mark 1:8 _____

Mark 1:14,15 _____

_____

Mark 1:17 _____

_____

Mark 1:32-34 _____

_____

Mark 1:35 _____

_____

Mark 10:45 _____

_____

How does the ministry of Jesus compare with what believers are to do today? (Mt. 28:19, 20)

_____

_____

The above passages indicate what the ministry of Christ was when He was on earth. It is also the ministry of the Body of Christ today. In other words, the ministry of Jesus Christ is a continuing ministry. It never stopped! It never will stop until the consummation of the age.

Now, here's the critical question: If God's ministry to the world is through Jesus Christ, and if God's ministry is to continue, who in the world is going to do it?

The Body of Christ—the Church

There is only one means for the work of God to be accomplished today. It is through the Church, the Body of Christ. Jesus said, "I will build my church, and the gates of Hades will not overcome it" (Mt. 16:18).

But what is the Biblical description of the Church? The Church is not a physical building, but a group of believers; not a denomination, sect, or association, but a spiritual Body. The Church is not simply an organization, but an organism, a *koinonia* (the Greek word for communion, or fellowship) that includes all believers.

Carefully read I Corinthians 12:12, 13, 27. Jesus Christ is now in this world in what form?

How do people become part of this living, spiritual Body? (vs. 13)

The work and ministry of Jesus Christ today is to take place through the lives of Christians, who together make up the Body of Christ. According to the Bible, Jesus is now physically at the right hand of God the Father in Heaven. The only way Jesus is presently manifested in the world is through:

Now, examine yourself! First, are you in the faith? Read II Corinthians 13:5. Is Jesus Christ really in you? Check one: yes ____ no ____ .

The rest of this course will be in vain if you are not spiritually alive and part of the dynamic work of the Holy Spirit in the world—who is doing the ministry of Jesus through you! If you are not sure, or believe you have not yet experienced a spiritual rebirth and new life in Jesus Christ, speak to your class instructor or another person whose spiritual wisdom you trust.

Second, are you continually filled with the Holy Spirit? In Ephesians 5:18 Paul specifically says, "be [continually] filled with the Spirit." It is not optional, but necessary and ongoing. It does not mean that we somehow receive more of the Holy Spirit at particular times (you received the Spirit when you believed in Christ—you can't receive *part* of a person). But it does mean that we are allowing the Spirit to have *all of us!* The

9

Spirit is allowed control of our lives. What are some evidences of being filled with the Spirit? (Eph. 5:15-21)

_____

_____

Paul tells us in Ephesians 4:30 not to "grieve" the Spirit. To grieve the Spirit is to cause sorrow or pain to the person and character of God the Spirit. By attitudes, actions, or disobedience, Christians can hinder the effectiveness of the Spirit's ministry in their lives. In what specific ways might Christians grieve the Spirit? (Eph. 4:29-32)

_____

_____

Paul also says that Christians should not _____ _____ (I Thess. 5:19). Some translations use the word "quench" to explain this sinful act. It also means to stifle, suppress, or to check the ministry of the Spirit through one's life.

The normal life-style for the child of God is to be _____ (Rom. 8:14). Look at Galatians 5:25 to find another phrase to describe this life-style: _____ .

Grieving and quenching the Spirit of God is sin, since it restricts the ministry of the Spirit through you. It must be repented of and confessed. But remember that God's love and grace have no limits. Even if you are struggling daily with a particular sin, God calls you to accept the fact that you are accepted in Christ. The Holy Spirit is constantly at work in you to bring spiritual renewal and growth—as you are open to it.

God's Ministers

You are now getting a glimpse of the awesome privilege and responsibility of being a Christian! The Church is made up of a body of ministers. Every Christian, every person who has the Holy Spirit dwelling in them, is part of the work and ministry of Jesus Christ in the world. A foundational passage giving this ministry perspective is II Corinthians 5:17-21. Read it carefully—at least twice. Now answer these questions:

According to verses 18 and 19, God has given each of us:

_____

From a dictionary, define the word "reconciliation."

_____

According to verse 20, we are actually Christ's:

_____

Our country appoints ambassadors to other countries to represent the American people and government. How would you say our assignment by God relates to the task of our government's ambassadors? What are we supposed to do?

_____

The Challenge

When you were a child, were you ever asked to do something that was simply impossible for you at your age? For example, were you required to drive the car at six, when you couldn't even reach the pedals? Of course not!

Now think for a moment about the awesome task God, your Heavenly Father, has given to you and to every Christian. You now represent Christ to the world. You are Christ's ambassador. You have been given the ministry of reconciliation by God Himself! You are responsible to continue the work of Jesus Christ on earth! Would God, your Father in Heaven, ask you to do something that is totally impossible for you? Would He mock you and frustrate you purposely with a "Mission Impossible"?

11

From Philippians 4:13 the clear answer to these questions is:

_____

Your spiritual gift is God's enablement for ministry and ambassadorship. The challenge is to be God's minister in the world. The enablement for this ministry is in finding and using your spiritual gifts in the power of God's Spirit!

Let's Get Personal

Do you believe you are already doing the ministry of Christ in some way? _____ Do you really want to be used by God and do His ministry? _____ Is your church doing the ministry of Jesus? _____ If not, what do you think God is saying to you about helping your church to more effectively be the Body of Christ to your community and the world?

_____

_____

At this early stage of the course, what changes do you think should take place in your life in order to do the ministry of Christ and be a real ambassador?

_____

_____

2

DISCOVER YOUR GIFTS!

A pastor was reviewing the membership rolls with one of the church boards. As they went down the list, the pastor wrote the initials FBPO by several names. After awhile one of the board members, too curious to hold back any longer, asked, "Pastor, what do those letters mean?" The pastor replied, "They mean, 'for burial purposes only.' You see, these are the inactive members!"

All Christians would be taken into Heaven's eternity immediately after conversion if God had no purpose for them on earth. There is a saying that has great Biblical backing, "We are saved to serve." There is no room for "deadwood" in the Body of Christ.

This lesson will help you understand spiritual gifts, how to discover your gift(s), and what hindrances might stifle your gift discovery and use.

What Are Spiritual Gifts?

Thayer, the famous Greek lexicographer, wrote in his *A Greek Lexicon of the New Testament* the following definition of spiritual gifts: "extraordinary powers distinguishing . . . Christians and enabling them to serve the church of Christ, the reception of which is due to the power of divine grace operating in their souls by the Holy Spirit." The Biblical word in the Greek language is *charisma* (plural = *charismata*) and means "gift of grace." Probably the best short, simple definition of spiritual gift is: the believer's Spirit-given ability for Christian service.

Spiritual Gift or Natural Talent?

Natural abilities (talents) are given to every person and are part of God's gift to all created beings. But spiritual gifts (abilities) are given only to those empowered by the Holy Spirit through rebirth. Therefore, we can say that everyone has talents, but only Christians have spiritual gifts.

Spiritual gifts function in the church—to build it up, or add to it—while natural talents function primarily in secular life. A person may have the spiritual gift of helps, and a natural talent for singing. Another person may be a talented singer who has the gift of exhortation. This latter person can have an especially powerful ministry through music, because his or her singing talent is enhanced by the spiritual gift of exhortation.

Believers must be careful to exercise spiritual gifts in the power of the Holy Spirit. Natural ability alone cannot generate a truly effective spiritual ministry, even though the outward circumstances may seem to indicate otherwise. Ray Stedman issues a helpful warning in his article "Equipped for Community" in *His* magazine:

The lesson is clear. Don't try to use your natural talents to accomplish the work of God, for talents cannot operate in that sphere. But use them as channels or vehicles for spiritual gifts, and you will find that they dovetail beautifully. You might expect that they would do this since they both come from the same God.

Who Has Gifts?

Some Christians secretly feel that they have no gift at all for spiritual ministry. Read I Corinthians 12:7 and I Peter 4:10. What does this passage say to a Christian who believes he or she has no spiritual gift?

_____

_____

If every Christian has at least one spiritual gift, what does this imply about gift use and development? Before answering, check I Peter 4:10, 11.

_____

_____

You are a gifted child of God! Since you have been gifted by God with ministry gifts, you should be aware that God has a sphere of service for every gift. List some possible areas in which your own gifts could function:

_____

_____

To sum it up, every child of God has received one or more gifts to be used for the upbuilding of the church. Sadly, not every believer is exercising his or her gifts— nor even knows what they are.

Gifts Are Varied

What would it be like for an athlete if part of his body, let's say his big toe, said "I'm not needed and I refuse to function"? Any athlete would be seriously hampered without part of his body functioning. The same is true for the Body of Christ! Not only is every part of the Body needed and necessary, but every part of the Body is different, too.

Read I Corinthians 12:4-26 and answer the following questions:

Though there are a variety of gifts, what are they all for? (vs. 7)

_____

15

Though there is great variety in the gifts, what is the common source? (vs. 11)

_____

Who decides what gift a Christian gets? (vs. 11)

_____

Why is there no room for boasting about spiritual abilities and ministry functions? (vss. 18, 21-26)

_____

_____

The implication is that no one can or should envy another's gift. To do so would be to imply that God didn't know what He was doing when He gifted us! What would happen if an orange tree tried to be an apple tree? What happens when a talented mechanic tries to be a musician when music is not his talent? In the same way, why do you think many Christians are frustrated with their particular ministry involvement?

_____

_____

Our point is that giftedness affects effectiveness in spiritual ministry. Because gifts are varied, so is effectiveness. However, lack of certain gifts does not allow any believer to ignore the clear commands of Scripture about living the Christian life in general. For example, the Bible tells us to pray for one another, whether we have the gift of faith or not. The Bible tells us to give and share our material possessions, whether we have the gift of giving or not. The Bible tells us to serve one another, whether we have the gift of helps or not. But those who possess such gifts will sense a special calling, ability, effectiveness, and joy in ministering within these areas.

Steps to Gift Discovery
A man told me of an old painting he had in his

basement. For years it collected dust and was unused. One day a friend, who knew art well, saw the picture in the corner and assured the owner that it was worth something. Surprised, but excited, the owner took the painting to be appraised and found it to be more valuable than he could have ever guessed. All the time he was much wealthier than he knew!

Many Christians live lives of spiritual poverty while they are unknowingly endowed with riches through Christ. Among those treasures are the spiritual gifts for ministry. How does the believer get the gifts out of his "basement" and into valuable function? Here are several steps to discovery and development of your gifts.

BE AWARE. Can you imagine a carpenter knowing how to build something without any understanding of his tools and how to use them? Every Christian must not only know what his or her spiritual resources are, but also what the gifts—and, especially, the *needs*—of the Body of Christ are. He can then begin to see how and where he fits into God's work.

Take time this week to familiarize yourself with the key New Testament passages on gifts: Romans 12; I Corinthians 12; Ephesians 4; and I Peter 4.

BEGIN MINISTERING. It is natural for the Christian to begin ministering and serving in some capacity. The New Testament is filled with commands to serve, teach, give, pray, witness, exhort, show mercy, etc. The well-known advertisement says, "Try it, you'll like it!" As you are open to the opportunities the Spirit may give, your gift will surface with power and effectiveness.

RESPOND TO DESIRES. One's gift, calling, and desires are often related. If you have a deep urge to become involved in a particular type of ministry and find an enthusiastic response to your ministry—it may be a sign that you have a gift in this area.

Note your desires and inclinations as you are involved in a ministry. Is God using you? Do you hunger for that activity or ministry? Are you surprised at your own effectiveness even though you didn't think you would do well? Your desires might be leading into areas where God has gifted you.

GIVE YOURSELF TO GOD. In Romans 12:1 the apostle Paul told the Romans to give themselves as a living sacrifice to God before he told them to use their gifts. As you become involved in ministries that give joy and satisfaction, make sure you are consciously giving yourself and those abilities to God for His use and service. As He blesses your ministry and multiplies it, you may see clear evidence of God's gifts working through you.

EXERCISE WHAT YOU HAVE. The apostle Paul told Timothy not to neglect the gifts he had. In other words, one should use and develop the gifts God has given. Just as muscles can atrophy through neglect and nonuse, so gifts can become dormant through neglect.

Some believers act as if they are ornaments on a Christmas tree. They look nice and they are present, but they apparently have no functional use. New Testament Christians are to be instruments in the hand of God. Through regular exercise (ministry) one's gifts can become stronger and more apparent to those who are helped by them.

ACCEPT AFFIRMATION. One of the best ways to discover your gifts is to see if they are recognized by others. As the believer ministers, he or she is affecting others. Others often are the best judges of true ministry.

Do others find help, encouragement, or spiritual uplifting through your ministry? What is their feedback and reaction to you and your ministry function? Think about past ministry involvement. What kind of feedback did you receive?

If you did not receive any feedback, why not talk with someone you respect? After doing this, record their responses below.

_____

_____

_____

_____

For the future, ask people whom you trust to observe you and give honest and regular feedback. Keep in mind, however, that many gifted and even famous Christians found that fellow believers did not recognize their gifts immediately—or perhaps their area of ministry was "behind the scenes"—apart from public scrutiny. But God is always aware of our work on His behalf! Don't depend *totally* on the opinions of others.

Conclusion

Review the six steps covered in this lesson to help you discover your spiritual gifts. Based on them, make a preliminary list of what you feel may be your gift or gifts.

_____

_____

_____

3

SPEAKING GIFTS:
APOSTLE, PROPHET

Imagine the Carpenter's shop holding a conference. As Hammer was presiding, several suggested that he leave because he was too noisy and rough. Hammer replied, "If I have to leave this shop, then Screw must go too. To accomplish anything with him, you have to turn him around again and again."

Screw then spoke up. "If you wish, I will leave, but Plane must go too. All his work is superficial; he has no depth."

To this Plane responded, "I think Rule will have to withdraw as well. He is always measuring people by his standards and thinks he is always right."

At this point, Rule complained about Sandpaper, "You should leave too because you are so rough and always rub people the wrong way."

As the discussion continued, in walked the Carpenter of Nazareth. Ready for a new day of work, He put on his apron and began to work on the new pulpit He was making from which the gospel would be preached. Throughout the day He used the hammer, screws, plane, rule, sandpaper and many other tools. At the end of the day's work, the pulpit was beautiful in its finished state. As the Carpenter's shop observed the finished product, Saw rose and remarked, "Brothers, I can see that we are all workers together with the Lord."

—Leslie Flynn, *19 Gifts of the Spirit*

This story reinforces the teaching of I Corinthians 12:14-26. Every part of the Body of Christ is important and essential to the health of the Church and the ministry of Jesus Christ. There is no room for pride, exclusiveness, or for feelings of inferiority or self-pity.

What Types of Gifts Are There?

The apostle Paul lists the gifts of the Spirit in three different chapters in three different epistles. Read Romans 12:3-8; I Corinthians 12:8-10, 28-30; and Ephesians 4:11. How many different gifts did you find? _____

Is this list exhaustive? Is it partial? Some believe that this is the complete list and that there are no other gifts. Others believe there are many more and that these were only some examples. Still others believe that while every possible spiritual gift may not be specifically mentioned, they all could be listed under one of the gifts mentioned by Paul. In this view, the Biblical gift list becomes an umbrella that covers a group of related gifts. For this study, we will examine 20 different gifts mentioned in the Biblical record. To assist your study they are divided into three categories: speaking gifts (those gifts primarily involved with verbal communication to others); serving gifts (those gifts that are primarily involved with acts of help and service to others); and sign gifts (those gifts primarily used by God to verify the authenticity of the messenger and the message).

I. The Gift of Apostle

The word "apostle" was used in two ways in the New Testament:

RESTRICTED USE. The original 12 apostles were unique according to the New Testament. What were some qualifications that made them special?

Mark 3:14 _____

_____

Acts 1:21, 22 _____

_____

Ephesians 2:19, 20 _____

_____

II Corinthians 12:12 _____

_____

The 12 apostles were unique for those reasons. This usage of the word was limited to the original apostles (I Cor. 15:7-9). When the apostles died, this restricted use of the office of apostle died with them.

GENERAL USE. Originally, in classical Greek, "apostle" meant one who was commissioned as the commander of a fleet of ships. One chosen as an apostle would possess great authority, stand under direct orders from the chief of staff, and be required to travel extensively, often in foreign lands.

The New Testament use was similar to this historical meaning. The word is derived from the Greek verb *apostello*, "to send." In Hebrews 3:1 it is used of Jesus as the Sent One of God; in Luke 11:49 of Jewish apostles sent by God to preach to Israel; and in II Corinthians 8:23 to those sent out by the churches.

Who are some other people called apostles in the Bible, who were not part of the original twelve but were obviously "sent ones" from Christ?

Acts 14:14 _____

Galatians 1:19 _____

I Thessalonians 1:1; 2:6 _____

Romans 16:7 _____

Romans 1:1 _____

An apostle was one commissioned by the Lord, sent into the world under orders, with a specific message from his superior. He was a messenger with authority.

As a spiritual gift, the gift of apostle would be defined as: the ability and responsibility to be sent by

22

Jesus Christ to communicate His Gospel and establish His Church, especially where it has not been before.

Discovering Your Gift

The following questions will help you determine whether you have this gift, or have an inclination toward it. After each question, mark a number according to how much this characteristic is evident in your life. Then add up your numbers and place the total in the spot designated.

0 = never true   1 = sometimes true
2 = regularly true   3 = almost always true

1. I have a desire to help start a work for God where it does not now exist. _0_

2. I believe God is calling me to be a missionary where there is a great need. _2_

3. I like to help organize and start new ministries. _1_

4. I have a regular compulsion to share the Good News with others and to encourage Christians to do God's work. _0_

5. I have a great concern for those who have never heard the Gospel and find myself thinking about going to them personally. _0_

6. I have had people encourage me to consider becoming a missionary. _0_

7. People have encouraged me to help start a new church or be a church planter. _0_

8. The idea of traveling to new areas to live and work is attractive and challenging to me. _1_

9. When God leads me to start something from scratch I can stick with it no matter what may interfere. _0_

10. I am good at visualizing something before it

23

becomes reality and tend to know how to make it happen. _0_

TOTAL: _2_

II. The Gift of Prophet

On the American scene, one of the most famous "prophets" is Jeane Dixon. She has made many predictions. In some cases she was amazingly correct and in others totally wrong. Is this kind of future-telling what we mean by the gift of prophecy?

Actually, foretelling the future is only a small part of the Biblical usage of the word prophecy. Our English word prophecy is made up of two Greek words that mean to "forthtell." A prophet is a person who tells forth or proclaims the message. In some cases Old Testament prophets did predict future events. However, the bulk of their message was aimed at pronouncing God's judgment upon religious and social wickedness, with God's promise of blessing to those who heeded the message. Right now, read through one or two of the Minor Prophets in your Bible to get a feel for the kind of preaching they did.

Now examine Exodus 4:10-16, a passage about Moses and Aaron, to see the function of forthtelling there. In what way is Aaron Moses' prophet?

_____

_____

In the Bible a prophet was God's spokesperson. He (or she—see II Chron. 34:22) was to be an instrument for instruction, warning, exhortation, promise, and rebuke. He was to speak to the historical, contemporary, practical conditions of the listeners. Both in the Old Testament and in the New Testament, the prophet was to speak the message of God to His people.

Thinking now of the specific New Testament gift, how did the gift of prophecy function? Let's examine some passages and be prepared to discuss them.

24

What was the purpose of the prophecy of Agabus, in Acts 21:10, 11?

_____

_____

What was the ministry of the prophets in Acts 15:32?

_____

Why is prophecy so important to the Church, according to I Corinthians 14:3, 4?

_____

_____

Some believe that the present-day gift of prophecy involves special messages from God beyond what is already found in Scripture, giving guidance and insight into every area of life. However, most Christian leaders have believed that God's new revelation has been completed and is found in the Bible. Until the New Testament was complete, the first-century prophets met the need that Scripture presently meets for God's people.

Yet, the Bible must be taught and applied to the specifics of each generation. The key ministry of the present-day gift of prophecy is to guide, strengthen, comfort, and encourage the believer with the truths of the Bible. The Holy Spirit takes the principles of the Bible and makes them living messages from God.

The spiritual gift of prophecy is defined as: the ability and responsibility to effectively speak God's message to people.

Discovering Your Gift

0 = never true   1 = sometimes true
2 = regularly true   3 = almost always true

1. I sense an inner urgency to persuade people to make spiritual decisions and commitments. __3

25

2. I find myself moved to challenge people with God's truth, to help them see how much God's Word and way can help them. _3_

3. When I share my testimony, I tend to point out some area of doctrine that has come alive to me through an experience or verse from the Bible. _2_

4. When evaluating another person's spiritual condition, I tend to point out or see the errors in his or her understanding of the Christian life. _3_

5. When I approach my personal devotions, I mostly prefer to relate to the verses emotionally, so as to get a personal blessing and application. _3_

6. If I have a choice of Bible passages to study, I mostly choose ones that are very practical. _2-3_

7. When called upon to serve, I am most naturally motivated to help in situations in which there are specific spiritual needs. _2-3_

8. When the opportunity comes up to counsel someone, I tend to give him or her the best Biblical solution I can think of. _3_

9. I have people tell me that they are encouraged, comforted, or edified by my talking with them or by my teaching/preaching. _1_

10. When I hear a poor sermon, I think of other ways to say God's words to these people. _3_

TOTAL: _26_

4

SPEAKING GIFTS:
EVANGELISM, SHEPHERDING

It's been said that when Nicolo Paganini willed his elegant violin to the city of Genoa, Italy, he demanded that it never be used. It was a gift designated for preservation, but not destined for service. How sad that an instrument so powerfully used for beautiful music would never again fulfill the function for which it was created!

When the resurrected Christ willed gifts to His chosen people, He commanded that they be used. They were functional gifts, not designed for preservation in human museums, but designed and destined for devoted service. How sad that some Christians have put their spiritual gifts on the shelf. How weakened the Church is by unused gifts that have such great potential!

We now turn to two other speaking gifts. Each is needed in the local church. Each has a special function to help perfect the Body of Christ to do its ministry.

The Gift of Evangelism

Evangelism means different things to different people. To some, evangelists are high-powered showmen or businessmen on television and radio who market a religious product. To others, they are enthusiastic religious fanatics who try to push their religion on people. To still others, evangelists are famous, respected preachers like Billy Graham, or those who simply live their faith by doing kind deeds and helping others.

What is evangelism? Who are evangelists? What is the gift of evangelism? The word "evangelism" itself does not occur in the Bible. In fact, it did not appear in the English language until the 17th century. The Greek word for "evangelist" only appears three times in the New Testament, in Acts 21:8; Ephesians 4:11 and II Timothy 4:5. Both words are derived from *euangelizomai*, "to announce the good news."

Though all Christians are to witness to their faith in Christ, the gift of evangelism is a special ability to communicate the Gospel message in relevant terms to unbelievers. For our purposes, the gift of evangelism is: the ability and responsibility to effectively communicate the Good News of salvation in Jesus in such a way that people respond and are converted.

The gift of evangelism involves four important aspects mentioned in the definition:

EFFECTIVELY COMMUNICATE. While it certainly includes works and life-style, the gift emphasizes a verbal witness so listeners understand the salvation message.

GOOD NEWS. What is proclaimed has historical content—including the historical reality of the life, death, and resurrection of Jesus Christ. The Greek word for "gospel" means good news. What is the Good News? It is the message that there is hope for humankind's guilt and alienation from God. There is peace with God through faith in Jesus Christ. There is salvation from the penalty of sin, the power of sin, and ultimately from the presence of sin.

PEOPLE RESPOND. Many people may be able to communicate the words of the Good News and still not be effective. The key to the spiritual gift of evangelism is that the Holy Spirit has made the Christian effective. People are converted.

28

DISCIPLESHIP. The process of evangelism isn't finished unless there is discipleship. What did Jesus command His disciples to do? (Mt. 28:19, 20)

Discovering Your Gift

0 = never true   1 = sometimes true
2 = regularly true   3 = almost always true

1. I have a consistent concern for people who don't know Christ and I would like to share the Gospel with them. 3

2. I enjoy sharing my faith when the opportunity arises. 1-2

3. I am at ease sharing with others how Christ is my Savior and Lord. 1

4. I am thrilled by the challenge and opportunity to share the Gospel with people I don't even know. 0

5. I find that people are open and listen to me when I share about my relationship with Christ. 1

6. I like sharing what Christ has done for me with both Christians and non-Christians. 2

7. Unbelievers understand and seem to respond when I explain who Jesus really is. 1

8. I get frustrated when I see that the church or other Christians don't seem to care as much about the lost as I do. 1

9. Some of the most joyful and fulfilling moments of my life have been leading others to Christ. 3

10. Even though I'm sometimes afraid, I still feel compelled to share my faith with those I meet, and I am amazed at how often they respond. 1

TOTAL: 15

The Gift of Shepherding

The word "pastor" occurs several times in the Old Testament—referring to leaders, kings, magistrates, who should be leading and caring for their "flock" of people. While the word "pastor" occurs only once in the New Testament (Eph. 4:11), the idea of the shepherd-leader occurs frequently in the New Testament (Jn. 21:16; Acts 20:28; I Pet. 5:2).

The word pastor (as we use it) most frequently refers to the office of pastor in the church. Every person called to the office of pastor should have the corresponding gift of shepherding. However, many Christians who do not have the office of pastor nevertheless have a gift for shepherding God's people. The Greek word from which a pastoral shepherding ministry comes is *poimen*. The Latin translation is *pastores*, from which we get the word "pastor."

What is the ministry of a shepherd as you see it in Jeremiah 3:15? _____

_____

In Jeremiah 23:4? _____

_____

Now look at John 21:15-17. What two-fold emphasis did Jesus give to Peter's ministry of shepherding God's "sheep"?

_____

Do you think that this is what all who have the spiritual gift of shepherding are called to do? Why or why not?

_____

_____

A person who has the shepherding gift functions in three ways. Take a few minutes to read Psalm 23. Write in your own words how the shepherding gift functions in these three areas.

Guiding _____

_____

Feeding _____

_____

Protecting _____

_____

According to Ephesians 4:12, the pastoring gift is one of those given to prepare God's people to find, develop, and use their gifts in ministry. They are to become equipped to be effective ministers. As Kenneth Gangel puts it in his book *Unwrap Your Spiritual Gifts:*

In addition to whatever else it may be, the gift of pastoring is a catalyst geared to release the gift potential of those in the flock. It also could be that the Holy Spirit, knowing the vast and diverse tasks of congregational care, equips pastors with several gifts to enable them to minister effectively as the shepherds of Christ's flock.

We have already seen however, that the gift of shepherding functions both in the office we call pastor, as well as outside that office. The shepherding gift is defined as: the ability and responsibility to spiritually guide, feed, and protect God's people.

Discovering Your Gift

0 = never true   1 = sometimes true
2 = regularly true   3 = almost always true

1. I have a desire to care for the spiritual welfare of new Christians. 2

2. I have a need to bring Christians together and help them grow and serve each other. 1

3. I find joy and fulfillment when I am responsible for the growth of a group of Christians. 1

4. I become concerned and protective when a Christian or a group of Christians is threatened by enemies of Christ. __+__

5. It is important for me to know, keep in touch with, and be known by those Christians I am responsible for. __

6. I have a strong desire to give myself to struggling or straying Christians so that they are encouraged and brought back into the group. __2__

7. I find that the Christians I work with and minister to are fed by my ministry and my application of Bible truths to their lives. __3__

8. People who have wandered from Christ or from the church body seem to respond well to my love and concern, and are often brought back. __0__

9. I seem often to be aware of the needs of a group of Christians I am with, and I would like to give guidance to the group if allowed. __4__

10. I feel frustrated if the church or a group of Christians isn't being cared for spiritually the way I know they could and should be. I sometimes wish I could do the job. __4__

TOTAL: __19__

5

SPEAKING GIFTS:
TEACHING, EXHORTATION

I once had the opportunity to visit a man dying of emphysema. The disease, which affects the lungs, kept him from getting enough oxygen. With every breath he hung precariously on the edge of life. It wasn't until I arrived at the hospital that I realized my chest cold would be life threatening to the patient. Recognizing my potential danger to the seriously ill man, I canceled the appointment until I was well. Though I wanted to help, I could have inadvertently killed him!

Great damage has been done by well-meaning but spiritually unhealthy Christians. With spasms of dedicated zeal, some of them have reached out into the world to help, while burdened with unsolved problems in their own lives. Unconsciously displaying hypocrisies, heresies, and inconsistencies, they have mocked Christianity in the eyes of those they hope to reach. The gifts of teaching and exhortation are designed by God to bring health, balance, and vigor to the Church.

The Gift of Teaching

Just as the shepherding gift reminds us of the earthly shepherding ministry of Jesus Christ, so an appreciation of the gift of teaching should lead us to think about Jesus as the Master Teacher. One who exercises the gift of teaching in the local church follows the pattern of Christ feeding His Church.

The gift of teaching is mentioned in three of the four major passages dealing with spiritual gifts: Romans 12:7; I Corinthians 12:28, 29 and Ephesians 4:11.

The concept of the *didaskalos* is a common but important one in the New Testament. Most people would agree that the chief function of the gift of teaching is to explain God's truth and how to apply it to life in a meaningful way for Christian growth. Teaching focuses on the written revelation of the Bible and how it is relevant to the present day.

Remember our discussion about the difference between talents and gifts? Both the talent of teaching and the gift of teaching have to do with the communication of truth in an organized way. But how do they differ?

- A talent is present from birth and may be developed. A gift is present from spiritual birth and may also be developed.
- A talent operates through grace given by God to all human beings. A gift operates through the special grace given believers in the Body of Christ.
- A talent may be applied to any subject it teaches. The gift of teaching communicates Biblical truths.
- Teaching talent yields understanding of the subject. The spiritual gift prepares for involvement in Kingdom work and obedience to the King.

The supernatural gift of teaching then, has the "spark" of God to enable the effectiveness of the teacher to edify and promote the spiritual growth of other believers. Usually someone with the talent of teaching has developed this ability through formal education. But a person with the gift of teaching, though he or she surely benefits from training and preparation, does not require formal education to communicate truth that the Spirit uses for building up believers.

Just about all Christians can do some teaching. What are some things people can teach who might not have the spiritual gift of teaching? (Heb. 5:11—6:1)

34

_____

_____

How might this help you discover your gift for teaching?

_____

In what ways was Ezra a model teacher? (Ezra 7:10)

_____

_____

What does Colossians 3:16 say about effective teaching?

_____

_____

Whether you have the gift of teaching or not, what warning is there for those who do teach? (Jas. 3:1)

_____

Discovering Your Gift

0 = never true	1 = sometimes true
2 = regularly true	3 = almost always true

1. I have a deep conviction that Scriptural truths should be understood and applied to daily life. _3_ _3_

2. I get excited about the meaning of words and truths of the Bible. _3_ _-3_

3. I am convinced that for Christians and the local church to grow there must be quality teaching and significant learning. _3_ _- 3_

4. I enjoy talking to either small or large groups, explaining the exciting truths of the Bible. _2_ _2_

5. When I need to prepare a talk or lesson for teaching, I am motivated to carefully organize the Biblical truths, so that the listener clearly understands them. _3_ _3_

6. When I read the Bible devotionally or for study, I

35

prefer to search out facts that add to my understanding of truth. 2-3

7. When I give a testimony, I tend to share some truth that has come alive to me through experience or verses I've read. 3-3

8. I seem to have the desire and the ability to dig into the Bible, search out the meaning of words and phrases, see how they fit into the great doctrines of the faith, and want to apply them to daily life situations. 2-3 -3

9. I seem able to explain well to others what the Bible and Christianity are all about. 2 -3

10. When I have the opportunity to teach or communicate Biblical truth to others, they seem to be spurred to growth in knowledge, attitudes, and actions. 1-2

TOTAL: 26   23 -28

The Gift of Exhortation

After spending three years with His disciples, Jesus announced His departure. This filled His disciples with fear and anxiety. To comfort and reassure them, Jesus told them of the "other Counselor" whom the Father would send (Jn. 14:16).

The Greek word used to describe the Holy Spirit is *paracletos*. It has two parts: *para*, which means "along side of," and *kaleo*, which means "to help," or "to comfort. Thus, the word means "one called alongside" to comfort and encourage. This same word is used in Romans 12:8 to describe the gift of exhortation.

The gift of exhortation then, is: the ability and responsibility to come alongside and provide encouragement, strength, stability, consolation, and help. Let's now examine some Biblical uses of the gift and ministry of exhortation.

What is one purpose of exhortation? (Acts 14:21, 22)

36

_____

_____

What is another use for the ministry of exhortation? (Acts 16:40)

_____

_____

How would exhortation help in the situation following the riot in Acts 19? (See Acts 20:1.)

_____

_____

As with any gift, there is a right and a wrong way to exercise the gift of exhortation. Check the following passages and see how this gift should be used.

I Thessalonians 2:11, 12 _____

_____

I Thessalonians 5:14 _____

_____

What is the source of spiritual exhortation? (Rom. 15:4)

_____

What do you think is the relationship of the gift of exhortation and the ministry of a spiritual counselor?

_____

_____

What are some different ways you could see the gift of exhortation used in your church?

_____

_____

Jot down the name of someone who needs encouragement, and plan how to reach out to that person.

_____

Discovering Your Gift

0 = never true   1 = sometimes true
2 = regularly true   3 = almost always true

1. I am accepting of people who seem to be deeply troubled or in a crisis. _1_

2. I am not only willing, but find fulfillment in being called alongside another person who is seeking encouragement, counsel, or challenge. _3_

3. When counseling another person, I tend to identify deeply with his or her situation and want to help them through it. _1_

4. When listening to others teach, I tend to get frustrated by studies that have little or no application. _3_

5. When I give a testimony, I tend to encourage or console others, rather than just share an experience or verse from the Bible. _1_

6. When talking with another Christian or in a group situation, I tend to challenge them to take certain actions to move ahead in their Christian walk. _3_

7. When reading the Bible for myself, I prefer to study passages with the purpose of changing specific areas of conduct or wrong attitudes. _2_

8. My reaction to the needs of others tends to be quick because I can usually sense what needs to be done and can tell them what they need to do. _3_

9. I find myself often encouraging those who are weak, wavering, doubting, or hurting in some way. _3_

10. I have a strong urge to verbally challenge those who are spiritually complacent and apathetic. _2_

TOTAL: _24_

6

SPEAKING GIFTS:
KNOWLEDGE, WISDOM

A small factory had to stop operations when an essential piece of machinery broke down. When none of the factory personnel could get it to function, an outside expert was called in for repairs. After looking the situation over for a few moments, the expert took a hammer and gently tapped the machine in a certain location. Immediately it began to run again. When the expert submitted a bill for $100, the plant supervisor went into a rage and demanded an itemized bill. When submitted, it read: "For hitting the machine, $1; for knowing where to hit, $99."

Knowing where, when, and how "to hit" is essential in today's church. Of course, we are not speaking of hitting machinery or people! But making crucial decisions in council meetings, the courage to give the appropriate word of caution or advice, the needed perspective for personal counseling or ministry changes— all these are very important ingredients of vital church life. The gifts of knowledge and wisdom help meet these essential needs.

The Gift of Knowledge

Today our culture is experiencing a "knowledge explosion," but this is not the same as the spiritual gift of knowledge. The gift of knowledge (I Cor. 12:8) is defined as: the supernatural ability and responsibility to investigate and systematize the facts and truths related to God's revealed truth. Through it, the Christian is enabled to acquire deep insight into divine truth. This gift helps us understand God's thoughts more deeply than would ever be possible using human reason alone.

Paul speaks of the "word" or "utterance" of knowledge because knowledge helps others only when it is communicated. Most Bible students would agree that this gift is closely related to the gift of teaching. With the gift of teaching, the emphasis is on the communication of truth, while with the gift of knowledge, the emphasis is on the knowledge or insight itself.

Most scholars would agree that in the early church the gift of knowledge was a revelatory gift. That is, it was used by God to reveal new truth to unfold His plan to the Church and to the world. As the canon of Scripture was completed, the gift of knowledge became primarily an interpretive gift, so that there is clear understanding of God's revealed truth.

Let's examine some passages in the Bible and see what we can discover about knowledge and how the gift functions in the believer's life and the church body.

What is the source of spiritual knowledge? (Prov. 2:6)

_____

What is a danger regarding knowledge? (I Cor. 8:1, 2)

_____

What comparison between knowledge and love is given in I Corinthians 13:8?

_____

How did Paul use his gift of knowledge? (II Cor. 11:6)

_____

Is this usage of knowledge intended to be a pattern for the Church? (II Cor. 2:14)

_____

What would you say is the difference between the gift of knowledge and formal education, where one receives much knowledge?

_____

_____

Read Colossians 1:9, 10. How would you say knowledge makes a difference or impact in the believer's life?

_____

_____

Discovering Your Gift

0 = never true   1 = sometimes true
2 = regularly true   3 = almost always true

1. I am motivated to study and learn Biblical truth and information. 2

2. Getting more knowledge about God, the Bible, and doctrine is exciting to me. 3

3. I would like to have a Biblical answer for everything possible—so much so, that I tend to study into matters deeply. 3

4. I have a great desire to share with others all these things I am learning and discovering. 3

5. I like to study issues and passages of Scripture that are difficult to understand. 2

6. When faced with having to counsel another person, I basically avoid discussions about feelings and instead prefer to share Biblical insights and truths. 3

7. If I have to teach or speak before another person or a group, I am most comfortable presenting a thorough, detailed study of a topic or passage from the Bible. 3

8. When serving in a church or Christian group, I am motivated to serve in areas where there are needs that challenge me intellectually. 1 2

9. Learning information and Biblical truths comes easily to me. 2-3

10. I have the ability to discover Biblical truths and principles by myself. 2

TOTAL: 23 - 24

The Gift of Wisdom

It is not enough to grasp, systematize, and understand deep truths of God. We must go on to relate those truths to the needs and problems of life. This is where the gift of wisdom is especially important and practical. As Leslie Flynn in *19 Gifts of the Spirit* says, "The ability to apply knowledge to vexing situations, to weigh their true nature, to exercise spiritual insight into the rightness or wrongness of a complex state of affairs calls for the gift of wisdom."

Knowledge stored in the mind is useless unless it is applied to the needs of life. Look for Biblical uses for the gift of wisdom from the following passages:

Matthew 10:18-20. _____

_____

Acts 17:16-34. _____

_____

Acts 6:1-7. _____

_____

I Corinthians 6:1-6. _____

_____

The gift of wisdom also applies to practical areas of life—such as marriage, dating, work, church life, eating, entertainment, life-style, money management, and so forth.

The Biblical word for wisdom in the original language is *sophia*. The definition of the gift of wisdom for our purposes would be: the ability and responsibility to interpret, demonstrate insight, and understand facts for godly application. A shorter definition could be, "the right use of facts to achieve the proper ends."

After reading I Corinthians 1:20-31, write down your thoughts distinguishing natural and spiritual wisdom.

_____

_____

_____

Discuss the characteristics of true wisdom from God, based on James 3:13-17.

_____

_____

_____

_____

What is the difference between knowledge and wisdom?

_____

_____

Can a person have and exercise the gift of wisdom without the gift of knowledge, or must one have both?

_____

_____

How would you distinguish between the gift of wisdom (I Cor. 12:8), and the wisdom for which we are to pray? (Jas. 1:5)

_____

_____

_____

Does the gift of wisdom apply only to spiritual matters or to all areas of life?

_____

Discovering Your Gift

0 = never true   1 = sometimes true
2 = regularly true   3 = almost always true

1. I have a great reverence for God and His purposes for all of life—including mine. 3

2. When faced with counseling another person I have some confidence because I honestly believe that God helps me to see solutions to others' problems. 3

3. I tend to be very effective at solving problems by using Biblical principles. 3

4. People seem to turn to me for ideas that are workable, for solutions to conflicting options, or for alternatives in discussions. 0 — 3

5. I do enjoy or would enjoy serving on a ruling or decision-making board since I like facing issues and seeing how they can be resolved for honoring God and helping God's work. 1 — 2

6. My reaction to the needs of others tends to be deliberate rather than responding emotionally, because I want to make sure the issues have been thought through. 3 — 2

7. I can readily see how Biblical truth should be applied to my life and to the lives of others. 3

8. It seems I am able to consistently make correct decisions for my life and family. 2 — 3

9. The advice I give to groups or individuals seems to work well. 1 —

10. My assessment of people, situations, and needs seems to be mostly correct. 3

TOTAL: 2)

SERVING GIFTS:
HELPS, HOSPITALITY, GIVING

We live in a society increasingly dependent upon verbal skills. Our society thrives on communication. Yet, every family, every person, and every society always needs those who are able to serve. Such support, often "behind the scenes" is essential to a thriving group—especially the local church.

The Gift of Helps

The gift of helps mentioned in I Corinthians 12:28 gains its name from the Greek word *antilempis*, which carries the idea of supporting, assisting, or lending a hand. According to Kittel, the famous Greek expert, it refers to the "activity of love in the dealings of the community" (*Theological Dictionary of the New Testament*).

Another word for the gift of helps is found in Romans 12:7. This word, *diakonia*, is where we get our commonly used word, "minister." Though the word has come to mean the "pastor" of a church, the concept applies to everyone in the church body. Everyone is to minister. Everyone is to help. (Note that *diakonia* is the same Greek word used in John 2 to refer to the servants waiting on tables at the wedding feast.)

Putting these two words together, we define the gift of helps as: the ability and responsibility to give assistance and support where a need appears.

45

If a person has a serving gift, how should he or she use it? (I Pet. 4:10, 11)

_____

Read Acts 9:36-39. Did Dorcas have the gift of helps? How do you know?

_____

_____

Read Acts 6:1-7 and describe the benefits and results of the operation of the gift of helps.

_____

_____

Is it possible to misuse the gift of helps? How might that happen in the church?

_____

_____

Discovering Your Gift

0 = never true   1 = sometimes true
2 = regularly true   3 = almost always true

1. When listening to a speaker, I am strongly impressed and want to respond to exhortations to serve other Christians. ___

2. In an organization, I prefer to be a follower with practical things to do to help make things happen and go smoothly. ___

3. When there is a task to do, I prefer to do it myself, rather than delegating it to someone else. ___

4. I find joy and satisfaction in taking on a helping role in some worthy project. ___

5. I prefer to be helping out in the background, rather than up front. ___

46

6. I am content to do menial jobs, or jobs others might consider unimportant. ___

7. Practical things like typing, cleaning, fixing, ushering, and other support tasks are meaningful and important for me to do. ___

8. I know key leaders can only do their job if someone takes over the supportive responsibilities. This is my place. ___

9. When called on to serve, I am most comfortable and motivated to help in situations of specific material needs. ___

10. When presented with a physical or spiritual need, I tend to respond best if the need does not require a lot of organizational detail or personal preparation. ___

TOTAL: ___

Gift of Hospitality

To understand this gift and its application to the Body of Christ, look at the history of the word "hospital." Leslie Flynn writes:

The main part of the word hospitality is hospital. Ancient travelers, whether pilgrims or businessmen, fared poorly when venturing beyond their own country. Thus, religious leaders established international guest houses in the 5th century. These havens were called "hospice" from hospes, *Latin for guests. With the coming of the Crusades, the importance of the hospice increased greatly. Pilgrims, crusaders, and other travelers found hospices, by this time run by religious orders, the only reputable guest houses of the era. Soon after the Crusades most of these institutions began to specialize in the care of the poor, sick, aged, and crippled. During the 15th century, secular interests took over most entertaining of travelers, so the hospital restricted its function to care and treatment of the sick and handicapped. But originally it meant a haven for guests.*
—19 Gifts of the Spirit

The Biblical Greek term for hospitality is *philoxenoi*, which is really a combination of two words. The first word means "love of" or "friendly to" (*philo*) and the second word means "strangers" (*xenoi*). The combination obviously means "the love of strangers."

The spiritual gift of hospitality has been defined as: the ability and responsibility to provide welcome, friendship, fellowship, food and/or lodging, especially to newcomers and strangers.

Based on I Peter 4:9-11, why do some see hospitality as a spiritual gift?

_____

_____

What command is given regarding hospitality, whether we have the gift or not? (Romans 12:13)

_____

_____

Why is it especially important for elders and other church leaders to be hospitable? (See I Timothy 3:2; Titus 1:8.)

_____

_____

Abraham can be cited as an example of showing hospitality to strangers in Genesis 18. What admonition is given in this regard in Hebrews 13:2?

_____

_____

Why, do you think, Peter urges us to offer hospitality "without grumbling" in I Peter 4:9?

_____

_____

Discovering Your Gift

0 = never true   1 = sometimes true
2 = regularly true   3 = almost always true

1. I get a lot of joy out of hosting people at my home who need ministry. __

2. I enjoy meeting new people and making them feel loved, accepted, and comfortable. __

3. Without worrying about the neatness or "readiness" of my home, I feel comfortable having people over to the house. __

4. It is fulfilling for me to see my home, my furnishings, and my food and household supplies used for those outside my immediate family. __

5. People seem to feel comfortable and at ease in my home, including those who need shelter and healing. __

6. I would be happy to add someone to my household temporarily in order to provide a helping hand or meet a need in their life. __

7. I am not threatened by strangers or new people—in fact, I find myself drawn to them to help them feel welcome. __

8. It would be a joy for me to host luncheons, dinners, or coffees for new residents in my area, or in my church. __

9. I show a genuine love and interest for each guest in my home or ministry group. __

10. I see my home as a haven for the lonely, the alienated, and the stranger. __

TOTAL: __

The Gift of Giving

The story is told of a man who was about to be baptized in a river. Suddenly he ran back out of the water, explaining that he had forgotten to give his wallet to his wife. The pastor called back, "Come on back with your wallet. We've already got too many unbaptized pocketbooks!"

It's been said that the most sensitive nerve in the human body is the one that leads to the pocketbook. Money is a touchy subject to many people. However, the Bible and Jesus Christ have much to say about money and our stewardship of our God-given resources. Paul writes in Romans 12:8, "If it [your gift] is contributing to the needs of others, let him give generously."

The tithe (or 10% giving) commanded in the Old Testament is a good beginning place for every believer. Christians who have been unusually blessed materially should be challenged to give much more than 10%. But the gift of giving is something above and beyond fulfilling the command to share and give of our resources. It is an inner urge, prompted by God, to give eagerly, joyfully, and without selfish motive to help others.

The spiritual gift can be defined as: the ability and responsibility to give materially to others and to the Lord's work with generosity and joy.

In Romans 12:8 we are told to exercise the gift of giving with *haplotes*. This word has been variously translated "simplicity," "single-mindedness," "liberality," and "cheerfulness." But the underlying meaning is to give to others and to God's work with "joyful eagerness."

Carefully read II Corinthians 9:6-14. What principles about giving do you see Paul teaching here?

_____

_____

_____

_____

Discovering Your Gift

0 = never true   1 = sometimes true
2 = regularly true   3 = almost always true

1. When presented with a physical or spiritual need, I tend to respond on my own initiative to try to meet it, especially through monetary or material generosity. __

2. With regard to financial matters, I am moved to give all I can to people and organizations I consider worthy. __

3. When called upon to serve, I am motivated to help in situations in which there are specific material needs like food, money, equipment, buildings, etc. __

4. I feel moved to help when confronted with urgent financial needs of others. __

5. I am often willing to sacrifice personal desires to give more generously to God's work. __

6. My convictions and my life show that all I own is really God's and is to be used for His glory. __

7. With regard to financial matters, I am concerned that God's money and ministry be used as efficiently as possible to accomplish more for people. __

8. I joyfully and cheerfully give to God's work and God's people. __

9. When I think about how much I love God, I want to give all the money and things I can to Him and His work. __

10. I manage my money well and restrict my standard of living in order to give liberally to God's work. __

TOTAL: __

SERVING GIFTS:
GOVERNMENT, LEADERSHIP

In his book *Unwrap Your Spiritual Gifts*, Kenneth Gangel relates an episode from the television series "Family Affair." Uncle Bill had planned a night out, and a baby-sitter was to arrive within minutes of Uncle Bill's departure to take care of Jody and Buffy until the next morning. The sitter failed to show up, which set the stage for an evening of high adventure for the two small children.

After a hilarious dinner of just what one might expect, Jody took over to tuck in his little sister for the night. As he turned out the light and prepared to leave the room, Buffy asked, "Who will tuck you in?" Displaying his newfound authority, Jody replied, "Nobody needs to. I'm in charge. Remember?" To which Buffy sighed and said, "I guess that's the trouble with people in charge. They have nobody to tuck them in!"

The people who have the gifts of government and leadership sometimes have "nobody to tuck them in." Yet, they are supernaturally enabled by God to fulfill an important function for the rest of the body, enabling the church to move forward with direction, unity, and purpose.

Some believe the gifts of government (some call it administration) and leadership are different aspects of the same gift. Others see them as two distinct gifts. For a long time I struggled with this issue, but now have arrived at the conviction that they are two distinct, but related gifts that equip others for ministry.

People often ask the difference between administration, management, government, and leadership. Many use these words in different ways. Business people tend to use the word management. Educators tend to use the word administration. For the sake of this study and for clarification, we will equate administration, management, and government.

Leadership will be placed in a different category. Leadership seems to be more identifiable by what a person *is*, while government seems to be more identifiable by what a person *does*. In other words, people can be leaders without being administrators, while others can be administrators without being leaders.

The Gift of Government

The Greek word for government is *kuberneseis*. The word means "helmsman," or "governor." The helmsman is the one who is qualified to steer the ship. This is the person who is gifted to give direction and set up the system to reach its desired goal. All its uses in Scripture refer to administration in some form of secular enterprise, except when the apostle Paul applies it to the church context.

All organizations need some form of administration. Though churches may have different names and roles, every church body has administrators to organize, direct, and channel its resources and people.

Read Acts 6:1-6. How does administration fit into this picture?

_____

_____

What should be the attitude of those who are in a position of government in the church? (Mk. 10:42-44)

_____

53

From Titus 1:5, what do you think was one of the things he was to "straighten out" among the churches on Crete?

_____

The gift of government might be defined as: the ability and responsibility to understand God's goals for a group or task and effectively organize the group to accomplish those goals.

Discovering Your Gift

0 = never true   1 = sometimes true
2 = regularly true   3 = almost always true

1. With regard to planning for the future of my church or organization, I tend to be concerned about and willing to do detailed work on the plans. __

2. I am able and willing to learn administrative skills such as planning, organizing, and delegating. __

3. I enjoy and am able to organize ideas, people, and projects for more effective ministry. __

4. If I am in a group meeting and there is no evident or assigned leader, I would want to appoint or ask someone in the group to lead. __

5. In terms of decision making, I often make decisions easily and with some degree of confidence. __

6. If asked to serve in a church or ministry program, I would tend to choose a position which involved detailed planning and decision making. __

7. I am able to lead a board, group, or committee in harmonizing various viewpoints to make a decision together. __

8. I enjoy leading and am able to recruit Christians to use their talents and gifts in ministry. __

9. I find great joy and fulfillment in organizing a

project or ministry so that others know what to do and are effective in doing it. __

10. People often look to me to set up procedures and plans to make changes or improvements of present ministries. __

TOTAL: __

The Gift of Leadership

Though Christ is the Head of the Church, the Holy Spirit works through individuals to provide direction, leadership, and guidance. This has been true in Old Testament history, in New Testament practice, and throughout the history of the Church. Christ appointed and trained the 12 disciples to give guidance and leadership to the early church. God continued to raise up leadership in the early church and leaders were appointed wherever churches were planted.

The Greek word for leadership is different from the word for government found in I Corinthians 12:28. The word for leadership in Romans 12:8 is *prohistemi,* which means "to rule," "to stand before," "to rank over." It applies to one who rules or presides over.

The gift of leadership is defined as: the ability and responsibility to sense and know God's goals for the church and to guide the body to the fulfillment of those goals.

This word appears eight times in Paul's writings and usually has the emphasis on personal leading of others and care for them. A key reference would be I Timothy 3:4, where managing or ruling one's own house and family is identified as a prerequisite for pastoral ministry.

A leader may not be highly gifted in the administration of the people and resources needed to achieve the goals. He or she may delegate the administration to another person, but he is able to get others to see the goals, want to achieve them, and move in that direction. For instance, Moses was a gifted leader, but he had to learn about administration from his father-in-law, Jethro. According to Exodus 18:13-26 what did Moses need to learn to do and why?

_____

_____

According to I Thessalonians 5:12, 13, how should those in leadership be treated by the church?

_____

_____

How should leaders treat those they lead? (I Pet. 5:1-3)

_____

According to Hebrews 13:7, what is the relationship between a leader's ability and his life-style?

_____

_____

Though someone may have the gift of leadership, there must also be "followership." What is the clear teaching of Hebrews 13:17 on this topic?

_____

_____

What would you say are some differences between leadership in the Body of Christ and leadership in the secular world?

_____

_____

_____

Name some areas in the life of churches that need leadership.

_____

_____

Discovering Your Gift

0 = never true   1 = sometimes true
2 = regularly true   3 = almost always true

1. In a group or organization, I prefer to lead. __

2. I am able to quickly assess the needs of a group and figure out how its goals should be accomplished. __

3. I enjoy and find it easy to motivate others to follow through on a ministry project. __

4. It's challenging and fulfilling for me to guide a group of people to achieve their desired goals and objectives. __

5. I almost automatically take responsibility or leadership when no other leaders have been designated. __

6. I have a strong desire to motivate others toward godly objectives. __

7. I usually know where we should be going as a group and can motivate others in that direction, too. __

8. I notice through my life-style, actions, and ideas, that I seem to motivate other Christians to follow me. __

9. Even in groups with different maturity levels, I seem to be able to lead with a positive response from the group. __

10. Generally speaking, I tend to be more sensitive to the overall organizational direction and goals, than to minority or individual opinions. __

TOTAL: __

SERVING GIFTS:
MERCY, FAITH, DISCERNMENT

Part of the work of Mother Theresa and the nuns associated with her in India is to pick up the dying from the streets of Calcutta and bring them to a building where they can die knowing someone cares for them. Many die; but some survive and are cared for. "We want them to know," Mother Theresa says, "that there are people who really love them, who really want them, at least for the hours that they have to live; to know human and divine love. There is always a danger, if we forget for who we are doing it. Our works are only an expression of our love for Christ. . . . To us what matters is an individual. . . . Every person is Christ for me."
—Kenneth Gangel, *Unwrap Your Spiritual Gifts*

The Gift of Showing Mercy

The popular song of the late 60's said, "What the world needs now is love, sweet love. It's the only thing there is just too little of." No one would argue with that. The Bible says that in the latter days society will be filled with love grown cold, with violence and brutality (II Tim. 3:1-4). Those with the gift of mercy have an unusual ability to show love to others. That's why a person gifted with showing mercy sparkles like a diamond against the background of society's indifference.

What attitude is to characterize the use of this gift? (Rom. 12:8)

Why is the emphasis of the gift on action, not just attitude? (Lk. 10:25-35)

The spiritual gift of showing mercy is defined as: the ability and responsibility to feel compassion for the hurting and to cheerfully take action to alleviate that hurt. The spiritual gift of mercy includes at least three characteristics:

A FEELING OF PITY. This is not just a temporary stirring of the emotions, but the deep-down, continuous compassion that is supernatural in origin. It is an extension of the compassion and graciousness of the Savior.

A DESIRE FOR ACTION. Beyond feeling pity, the mercy giver will not rest until something is done to alleviate the hurt. Jesus' compassion was always followed by action—whether in healing, feeding, or on the cross. In this connection, what does James 2:15, 16 say about compassion?

AN ATTITUDE OF CHEERFULNESS. The attitude with which we help a person conveys as much or more than the action itself (Rom. 12:8). A joyful, cheerful, positive attitude in mercy ministry is evidence that God is its source.

Discovering Your Gift

0 = never true   1 = sometimes true
2 = regularly true   3 = almost always true

1. I feel deeply and hurt for others who are sick, imprisoned, poverty-stricken, or broken in some other way. _2_

2. When faced with counseling another person, I tend to deeply identify with his or her situation. _1_

3. When I choose Bible passages to study, they are very practical ones. *2*

4. Generally speaking, I tend to help meet obvious needs without measuring the worthiness of the needy person or evaluating what the real needs may be. *1*

5. I have a strong desire to do acts of love and kindness for those who cannot or will not return them to me. *2*

6. I find fulfillment and contentment in meeting the needs of the suffering or the undeserving. __

7. I cheerfully do tasks others find distasteful in order to minister to suffering and desperately needy people. __

8. I enjoy being an agent of blessing to those in hospitals and nursing homes. *1*

9. Even though people may bring problems on themselves and even justly deserve it, God uses me to help them and spare them some of the consequences. *2*

10. In situations requiring organizational decision making, I tend to lack firmness because I am more concerned for people's feelings. *2*

TOTAL: *5*

The Gift of Faith

The gift of faith listed by Paul in I Corinthians 12:9 is more than saving faith. No one can begin the Christian life without exercising genuine faith in Christ's saving work (Eph. 2:8). Faith is likewise needed as we continue growing in the Christian life (II Cor. 5:7). However, not all Christians possess the faith that moves mountains. The gift of faith (I Cor. 13:2) is the Spirit-given ability to see something that God wants done and to sustain unwavering confidence that God will move to do it, even when faced by seemingly insurmountable obstacles.

The author of Hebrews describes faith in very specific terms. According to Hebrews 11, what is faith?

_____

How is this gift of faith different from the faith every Christian has? Kenneth Gangel describes it this way:

The person who demonstrates the gift of faith is characterized by utter dependence on the Lord. He puts little stock in human resources; and even when they are available, he realizes that God has indirectly supplied them through the human donor. The Christian with the gift of faith is able to see what others cannot see, to endure what others cannot endure, and to genuinely trust God when there seems to be no human or natural basis for that trust.
—*Unwrap Your Spiritual Gifts*

We would define the gift of faith as: the ability and responsibility to confidently discern the will and purpose of God for His work and believe that God will accomplish it, even when it looks impossible.

What part is faith to have in the life of every Christian?

_____

Hebrews 11:6 _____

Colossians 2:6 _____

Romans 14:23 _____

The gift of faith seems to be a special kind. Read I Corinthians 12:9 and 13:2. How do you see the gift of faith as being beyond the "typical"?

_____

_____

Read Mark 11:22-24. How did Jesus challenge His disciples about faith?

_____

_____

How could those with the gift of faith help the rest of us grow in our faith?

_____

_____

What is the relationship of faith to love? (I Cor. 13:2)

_____

Discovering Your Gift

0 = never true   1 = sometimes true
2 = regularly true   3 = almost always true

1. Usually, I have a tendency to visualize God's goals for His work. Then I work toward them despite roadblocks. __

2. I am convinced that God answers prayer and that He works specifically through my prayer life. __

3. I feel great satisfaction and joy in persisting through prayer for specific needs. __

4. It seems that I depend on God's resources and guidance much more than most others. __

5. I get excited about and feel at ease around others who pray much for situations and people needs. __

6. What appears impossible to others, seems possible to me because God can do it. __

7. I am convinced that, despite circumstances, God is going to keep His promises, and my life shows it. __

8. When I feel that God has led, I seem to have unusual assurance that it will be accomplished, no matter what. __

9. When planning for the future of my church or Christian group, I am more concerned with seeing the end results than with concerning myself with the details of getting there. __

10. I tend to encourage other Christians to trust God and think big in terms of certain goals and actions. ___

TOTAL: ___

The Gift of Discernment

Everyday someone in this country sells good merchandise for worthless currency. The money looks and feels like legal tender, but it's counterfeit—phony and worthless. A whole office in the U.S. government, the Secret Service, is trained in discerning the fake and tracking down the counterfeiters.

The special ability to find spiritual counterfeits is the Spirit-given gift of discernment. Human philosophies, cults, sects, and hypocrites run rampant in society and even in churches. Without the gift of discernment operating in the Church, Christians can be deceived and entrapped by false teachers and their doctrines.

The gift of discernment is defined as: the ability and responsibility to distinguish between the spirit of truth and the spirit of error.

Carefully read II Corinthians 11:13-15. How does Satan disguise himself in the Church?

_____

What does it mean to masquerade as a servant of righteousness?

_____

What are some major issues concerning which Christians should exercise discernment, based on the following passages?

I John 4:1 _____

I John 2:18; 4:3 _____

Galatians 1:6-9 _____

Acts 20:28-31 _____

I Corinthians 6:1-7 _____

Discovering Your Gift

0 = never true   1 = sometimes true
2 = regularly true   3 = almost always true

1. I tend to probe and analyze to determine other Christians' true spiritual condition or needs. __

2. Generally, I tend to be wise in discerning the personality, character, and spirituality of others. __

3. Usually I am able to detect weaknesses and pitfalls when evaluating opportunities and situations. __

4. I am often able to see through others' actions and know their real motives and inner attitudes. __

5. There are times when I sense a particular teaching is unbiblical or off-balance. __

6. I believe I am able to differentiate between demonic influence and mental illness. __

7. I seem to be able to judge well between the evil thing and the good thing, as well as the acceptable and the unacceptable. __

8. In Christian, as well as secular environments, I am able to detect error and false teaching and relate it to truth. __

9. Usually I can spot a phony person before others do. __

10. Other Christians seem to look to me for insight into the truthfulness of a particular teaching or person. __

TOTAL: __

SIGN GIFTS:
MIRACLES,
HEALINGS

Water turned to wine; children and adults raised from the dead; eating poison and not being harmed, walking across raging flooded streams, cancerous tumors disappearing, once blind eyes able to see . . . . From Indonesia, Nigeria, Brazil, the United States and many other parts of the world—reports come of signs, wonders, and miracles. Are these true, counterfeit, or fake? Are they of God, Satan, or charlatans?

It is impossible to consider Christianity without considering miracles. God is a God of miracles. Beginning with Moses and throughout the Bible, we see that God performed miracles through His people and for His glory. The sign gifts are those gifts that reflect the obvious supernatural intervention of God in the natural order and processes of life. They have a three-fold purpose:

1. To display the power of God so that observers are confronted with the reality of God's awesome might. Example: Psalm 77:13-15. How was God's might demonstrated in the miraculous events spoken of here?

_____

_____

2. To demonstrate the authority of the messenger and of the message being carried. Example: Acts 13:6-12.

How was the miracle in this case used to demonstrate the authority of the messenger?

_____

3. To cause people to listen to God's message. Example: Mark 2:3-12. How did this miracle cause people to listen to God's message?

_____

_____

Sign gifts, then, are especially used of God as He chooses to minister to the Body of Christ and to alert unbelievers to the reality of God and of His message.

There is confusion today however, on the availability and frequency of these gifts. There are two extremes this study wishes to avoid. One extreme is to categorically deny the present-day existence of sign gifts. The very definition of a miracle assumes divine intervention into the ordinary course of nature. Surely God is able to do this at any time.

The other extreme is the frequently heard teaching that any person, at any time, can and should be able to do miracles and signs in the name of Jesus. This was never true in Biblical times, nor is it true today. The Scripture is clear that only certain believers were gifted by God with sign gifts.

Did all great men of God do miracles? (See Jn. 10:41.)

_____

Who were the ones to perform signs, wonders and miracles and how did the rest of the believers feel about them? (Acts 5:12, 13)

_____

_____

What were the special marks of a first-century apostle? (II Cor. 12:12)

Sign gifts can still be used by God today if He so chooses. However, sign gifts have a specific purpose and are used by a sovereign God through His chosen vessels. In some places and times they may be highly visible. On other occasions they may be totally absent.

The Gift of Miracles

The definition of the gift of miracles is: the ability and responsibility to authenticate God's Word through supernatural acts. There are three primary Greek words for miracle: *dunameis* (power), *terata* (wonder), and *semeis* (sign). Examples of the use of all three of these words for miracles can be found in passages like Acts 2:22. However, the point of all miracles is faith in God, and specifically, in His Son Jesus Christ. (See Jn. 20:30, 31.)

Leslie Flynn in his book *19 Gifts of the Spirit* basically defines miracles in three ways, according to the three words used in Scripture for the miracle. Let's look at them:

POWER. God has set down natural laws by which His universe runs in order. A miracle is God's supernatural intervention into the laws of nature, causing the natural course of events to be interrupted or by-passed in some way.

WONDER. To qualify as a miracle it must be observed, eliciting feelings of awe, making people wonder in amazement. (For examples, see Mk. 2:12; Mk. 6:51; Lk. 5:9.)

SIGN. The power of a miracle authenticated the doer of the miracle as a divinely commissioned servant of the Lord. The message is validated by the miracle. The prophets, Jesus, and the apostles backed their messages by miracles from God.

Miracles seemed to abound in the New Testament days. Many ask the question, "Why do miracles seem to be rare today, and the gift of miracles even rarer?" There are several answers to this important question.

TRUE MIRACLES FROM GOD ARE ORDAINED AND CONTROLLED BY GOD. He can choose when and where to send them. There have been long periods of Biblical history with few or no miracles. It seems God chooses certain times in history to be more active with miracles (the beginning of the Christian Church, in Acts, for instance). Many believe we are now entering a time preceding the culmination of history when miracles will again be common.

THE UNBELIEF OF PEOPLE MAY BE ANOTHER REASON. We know that Jesus did no miracles in certain towns because of the people's unbelief and resistance to God. Perhaps the Western mind-set has focused on the rational and the scientific to the point of excluding God from people's expectations. Many act as if God can not, or will not do a miracle. This expectation is fulfilled.

OTHERS SAY IT IS BECAUSE OF THE NEED. They note that miracles seem to be much more common in "primitive" situations where the Word of God is not in written form, or available in other ways. Miraculous verification is more necessary in these cases, some would say. Many third-world cultures need their senses awakened to the Gospel by the miraculous because they have seen miracles done by the power of Satan. They need a clear demonstration that the power of God is greater, as in the case of Moses when he was before Pharaoh.

What was the primary purpose of New Testament miracles? (Jn. 20:30, 31)

What do some people need before they believe in Christ? (Jn. 4:47-53)

How does Jesus characterize those who chase after miracles and signs from God? (Lk. 11:29)

_____

Do you believe that the gift of miracles is given today? Why or why not?

_____

_____

How should we relate to Christians who greatly differ from us in their view of miracles for today?

_____

_____

Discovering Your Gift

0 = never true   1 = sometimes true
2 = regularly true   3 = almost always true

1. I have been amazed (and so have others) by miracles God has done through my life for the good of others. __

2. God has broken natural laws in answer to my prayers. __

3. As God does miracles through my life and words, people come to faith in Christ and believe the Gospel. __

4. When a situation seems humanly impossible, God gives me faith and confidence to speak or act so that a miracle transpires and people are helped. __

5. When asked to serve in a ministry or leadership capacity, I tend to get involved in situations that require great faith in God and absolute miracles. __

6. God has caused many people to come to Christ who otherwise seemingly would not, through miracles God has done through me. __

7. When God does a miracle through my ministry, it is

so obvious that people are in awe of God and wonder at His power. __

8. I find great joy in seeing God's miracles work through me so that people have greater faith in God. __

9. In situations where nothing would convince people that God is real, I have seen Him do miracles through me. __

10. I know that nothing is impossible with God and have seen evidence of that through specific miracles in my ministry for God. __

TOTAL: __

The Gifts of Healing

Normally, people speak of the "gift of healing" (singular) and usually mean by it, physical healing. However, the gifts of the Spirit are all referred to in the singular, except for this gift, the "gifts of healings" (I Cor. 12:9). Because the Scripture speaks of spiritual, emotional, and physical healings, I believe that the "gifts of healings" refers to these different levels and types of healings.

The gift of healing, then, is defined as: the ability and responsibility to make sick people well. Basically, the person with the gift of healing is used of God to intervene in a supernatural way, as an instrument of God, for the curing of some type of illness and the restoration of health.

Remembering that all the gifts of the Spirit are meant to carry on the work of Jesus Christ, take a look at the following passages. Jot down what characterized Jesus' healing ministry.

Matthew 9:34—10:1 _____

Matthew 4:23, 24 _____

Matthew 8:1-3 _____

Matthew 8:5-13 _____

Matthew 12:11-13 _____

Matthew 14:35, 36 _____

Matthew 15:30, 31 _____

Matthew 17:14-18 _____

Since there has been much misunderstanding regarding this gift and its use, it is important to note that the gift of healing is subject to some restrictions:

NOT ALL SICKNESS IS HEALED BY THE GIFT OF HEALING. People will still die. It's been facetiously said, "The gift of healing heals every disease but the last one." For instance, Paul clearly had the gift of healing (Acts 14:8-10), yet, in what instances did he not heal someone?

Philippians 2:25-27 _____

I Timothy 5:23 _____

II Timothy 4:20 _____

THE FAITH OF THE SICK PERSON IS NOT ALWAYS A KEY TO HEALING. Some people have great faith that God will heal them, but He doesn't. Others had no evidence of faith, yet God chose to heal them anyway (Acts 3:1-8). While some sickness is due to a person's sin and disobedience (I Corinthians 11:30-32), most sicknesses have nothing to do with a person's personal responsibility. Explain why the man in John 9:1-3 was sick.

_____

_____

THE GIFT OF HEALING DOES NOT EXPLAIN ALL HEALINGS. This is true in the same way that the gift of giving does not account for all giving, or the gift of teaching account for all teaching. God can choose to heal someone through any believer's prayer.

One must understand that some healing may be demonic and some healing may simply be psychic. In the first century there were many demon-energized healers and magic workers (Acts 8:9-13; 13:6-11) as there doubtless are today. I believe however, that the gift of healing has never been totally taken away from the Church, even though there has been an abundance of fraud and deceit in the Church over the centuries.

GOD MAY CHOOSE NOT TO HEAL A PERSON FOR SEVERAL REASONS. As mentioned earlier, some diseases are for personal discipline (I Cor. 5:5; 11:28-32). According to II Corinthians 12:7-9 why do you think God didn't remove Paul's "thorn in the flesh"?

_____

Sometimes God uses our physical ailments to add empathy to our ministry so we can comfort others (II Cor. 1:3, 4). Look up John 9:2, 3 to find one more reason why God allows us to be ill.

_____

What should a Christian who does not have the gift of healing do when someone is sick?

_____

Are all healings from God the same as this gift?

_____

_____

Is it God's will for all Christians to be healed? Why or why not? Back your answer with Scripture.

_____

_____

Discovering Your Gift
0 = never true   1 = sometimes true
2 = regularly true   3 = almost always true

1. When given ministry opportunities, I tend to accept ministries where there are hurting or sick people that God can heal through me. __

2. God has used me to bring physical healing to others above the natural healing processes. __

3. God uses me to bring healing to those who are emotionally sick. __

4. I am strongly drawn toward those who are ill with different types of diseases and sicknesses, and know that God can heal them through my ministry. __

5. I have seen people come to Christ and/or be strengthened in their faith through healing God has accomplished in their lives through my ministry to them. __

6. When reading passages in the Bible describing healing, I can identify with them, because I have seen them similarly accomplished in my ministry. __

7. I am deeply concerned for those who are ill in any way and am bothered that the church doesn't do more to bring healing to them. __

8. God uses my prayer and/or healing touch to bring healing to others. __

9. Other Christians seek me out for prayer when they sense a need for healing. __

10. Though not everyone is healed, I see God miraculously healing individuals through my ministry to them. __

TOTAL: __

11

SIGN GIFTS:
TONGUES,
INTERPRETATION

One of the most controversial and significant developments in the history of twentieth-century Christianity is the growth of the "tongues movement." Four stages are recognized in the development of what is called the "charismatic movement."

Stage one was the outbreak of tongues speaking in Los Angeles in 1906 with the subsequent establishment of small Pentecostal denominations. These grew and spread slowly in the early part of the century.

Stage two was the acceptance of speaking in tongues in the mainline denominations beginning about 1960. Many people believe this openness was due to the lack of spiritual vitality in the mainline churches.

Stage three was the sudden and massive infusion of the "pentecostal experience" in the Roman Catholic Church in the mid and late 1960's. This change brought to many Catholics a greater emphasis on one's personal relationship with Christ, the ministry of the Holy Spirit, and the need to return to New Testament Christianity.

Stage four is the more recent widespread recognition that God can and does continue to work in miraculous ways. These miracles are not confined to the traditional framework of Pentecostal denominations that stress a second experience of the Holy Spirit, commonly called the "baptism of the Holy Spirit." Currently there is widespread recognition across many denominational lines that God has given all of the gifts to the Church and they can be exercised in an appropriate and Biblical way without falling into the misuse discussed by the apostle Paul in I Corinthians 12—14.

What Is the Gift of Tongues?

The technical word for the gift of tongues is the English word "glossolalia," which comes from the Greek word *glossa*, meaning "language." The gift of tongues is not mentioned often in the Scriptures, but it is mentioned in the Book of Acts, chapters 2, 10, and 19, and in I Corinthians chapters 12—14. There is disagreement as to whether the tongues were actually known languages or ecstatic utterances which communicated spiritual truth.

Check the following passages and be prepared to discuss your answers in the group meeting.

Read Acts 2:1-4 and describe what happened.

_____

_____

What indication is there in Acts 2:5-8 that this gift was of known languages?

_____ _____

How does this relate to Paul's use of his gift of tongues, spoken of in I Corinthians 14:18, 19?

_____

Based on this study of Scripture, we would define the gift of tongues as: the ability and responsibility to speak in a language which has not been learned.

What Is the Purpose of Tongues?

Look again at Acts 2:1-11. What seems to have been the purpose of the apostles speaking in tongues at this time?

_____

What was the purpose of tongues in Acts 10:44-46?

_____

In Acts 19:1-7?

_____

How do your answers compare with I Corinthians 14:22?

_____

As with the other sign gifts, it seems that the purpose of the gift was evidential, that is, it authenticated the message of the apostles and gave a springboard for evangelizing the hearers. In the Book of Acts, we see the gift of tongues used as a major breakthrough to three groups of distinct people. What group of hearers was affected in Acts 2:1-13?

_____

According to Acts 10:44-47 what distinct group of people came into the Church?

_____

Now look at Acts 19:1-7. What special group entered a new relationship with the Church?

_____

What Are the Biblical Guidelines?

The exercise of this gift has not been unaccompanied by problems—even in New Testament times. No spiritual gift is ever to be used to bring attention to the one using the gift; but to glorify God, who is the source of the gift. In the church at Corinth, individuals were using the gift to edify themselves. At this level, no gift can function properly. Hoping to correct this abuse, Paul gave several guidelines regarding the exercise of this gift. Look at I Corinthians 14:26-28. What three principles do you find?

1. _____

2. _____

3. _____

Check verse 23 to find what Paul said was likely to happen if these guidelines were not followed.

_____

Because of misunderstandings that have plagued this gift since New Testament times, it is vital to understand these basic principles:

THE BAPTISM OF THE HOLY SPIRIT IS NOT ALWAYS INDICATED BY THE ABILITY TO SPEAK IN TONGUES. According to I Corinthians 12:13, what does the Spirit's baptism do?

_____

According to I Corinthians 12:27-31 are all believers to speak in tongues?

_____

When does the Spirit enter a Christian? (Eph. 1:13, 14)

_____

There are some groups that teach that the key evidence of the baptism of the Spirit is the gift of tongues. What is your view, and that of your own church?

_____

_____

THE GIFT OF TONGUES IS NOT A REQUIREMENT FOR SPIRITUAL GROWTH. If it were, the Bible would be full of exhortations to seek this gift so one could grow in Christ. According to I Peter 2:2, what is the Biblical method of growth?

_____

TONGUES ARE NOT NECCESSARILY A SIGN OF SPIRITUAL MATURITY. It is possible to have this or any other gift and be living a carnal Christian life. The church that caused the apostle Paul more grief than any other was the Corinthian church. It was marked by immaturity, immorality, and pride. Yet, what gifts did the Corinthians have? (I Cor. 1:7)

And how did Paul address them? (I Cor. 3:1)

THE GIFT OF TONGUES DOES NOT BUILD UP OTHER BELIEVERS UNLESS IT IS USED WITH INTERPRETATION. The gifts that especially build up the church are those that can be understood—those that encourage and edify the Body of believers. Look at I Corinthians 14:13. What should a person who has the gift of tongues pray to be able to do?

THE ABILITY TO SPEAK IN ECSTATIC LANGUAGES IS NOT LIMITED TO CHRISTIANITY. It is practiced among the Hindus, Mormons, and different tribal religious groups in third-world countries. This fact has helped Biblical Christians recognize that tongues can come from three sources: the Holy Spirit, psychological inducement, and Satanic influence. Believers must discern the difference and stress the need for interpretation of tongues.

Discovering Your Gift

0 = never true   1 = sometimes true
2 = regularly true   3 = almost always true

1. I have the ability to speak a language I don't understand. __

2. Through interpretation of what I say, I can tell of God's goodness and salvation in a language I never learned. __

3. Others have been helped and drawn to Christ

78

through a language I can speak but which I don't understand. __

4. Though I can't understand this language, I know that I am saying God's words and doing His will. __

5. When I have spoken an unknown language in the presence of other Christians, it has been interpreted as words of help and encouragement from God. __

6. Sometimes I just want to praise and thank God and find myself saying words I have never heard or learned before. __

7. When I speak in this new language I feel fulfilled and blessed—as if God has spoken to me and through me. __

8. When I speak in this new language I have great confidence and assurance that God is speaking through me to others. __

9. I have had people come to faith in Christ by hearing this language and its interpretation. __

10. I have had unusual experiences using this unknown language, especially desiring to speak it to people I don't know so that they may be able to know about Christ. __

TOTAL: __

Interpretation of Tongues

The Greek word *hermeneuo* means to "explain, interpret, and translate." We define this gift as: the ability and responsibility to hear words spoken in tongues and then communicate those words in a language listeners will understand. Your understanding of this gift may develop as you examine the following passages.

Why is the interpretation of the gift of tongues so important? (I Cor. 14:4)

_____

_____

Is the gift of interpretation given to the same person who has the gift of speaking in tongues? Explain, based on I Corinthians 12:10; 14:5, 13, 27, 28.

_____

_____

What should be done if there is no one to interpret for those who would speak in tongues? (I Cor. 14:28)

_____

Is there significance in the fact that there is no record of Jesus speaking in tongues? If so, what do you think it is?

_____

_____

What is your position on the gift of tongues and its use today? Why?

_____

_____

Discovering Your Gift

0 = never true   1 = sometimes true
2 = regularly true   3 = almost always true

1. God has given me the ability to understand and speak forth His truth from languages I have never learned before. ___

2. When someone speaks in tongues, I have an overwhelming urge to say what it means and be confident that it is right. ___

3. I have seen people encouraged and blessed when I interpret the tongues language another Christian is speaking. ___

4. Though I don't know the language, I seem to know what someone is saying when he or she speaks in a language others don't know. ___

5. I believe I am God's spokesperson when I am interpreting a message in an unknown language given by another person. __

6. When someone is speaking in a God-given language, I hear them praising God and telling of His great works. __

7. It gives me great joy to interpret the words of another Christian who is speaking in tongues. __

8. God uses me as an interpreter of languages so that others can be helped. __

9. Sometimes when I interpret tongues, I find that others come to faith in Christ through the message I give. __

10. Other Christians and the church look to me to interpret a God-given language that someone is speaking. __

TOTAL: __

12

HOW DO I KNOW?

Bill Bright tells the story of a famous oil field known as Yates's Pool:

During the depression this field was a sheep ranch owned by a man named Yates. Mr. Yates wasn't able to make enough on his ranching operation to pay the principal and interest on the mortgage, so he was in danger of losing his ranch. With little money for clothes or food, his family (like many others) had to live on government subsidy.

Day after day, as he grazed his sheep over those rolling West Texas hills, he was no doubt greatly troubled about how he would pay his bills. Then a seismographic crew from an oil company came into the area and told him that there might be oil on his land. They asked permission to drill a wildcat well and he signed a lease contract.

At 1,115 feet they struck a huge oil reserve. The first well came in at 80,000 barrels a day. Many subsequent wells were more than twice as large. In fact, 30 years after the discovery, a government test of one of the wells showed that it still had the potential flow of 125,000 barrels of oil a day. And Mr. Yates owned it all. The day he purchased the land he had received the oil and mineral rights. Yet, he'd been living on relief. A multimillionaire living in poverty! The problem? He didn't know the oil was there, even though he owned it.

—Bill Bright, founder and president of Campus Crusade for Christ International, in *How to Be Filled with the Holy Spirit.*

Many Christians, sadly, have a similar problem. They live in spiritual poverty, unaware of the potential that God has given to them to do His great, divine ministry! They are unaware of the gifts that the Holy Spirit has given them for use in God's eternal work.

This lesson seeks to further answer the significant question of which gifts for ministry you may have.

How to Discover Your Gifts

We have already discussed some ways of going about gift discovery in Lesson 2. Now, after studying each of the gifts, let's look at this again.

1. Make sure you are a Christian. When you were born physically, you received certain physical traits. When you are born spiritually, you receive spiritual traits, including your spiritual gifts. Jesus said, "You must be born again," (Jn. 3:7). If you are not sure you have been born spiritually, speak to your study leader about this and settle this essential life issue.

2. Offer your life as a sacrifice for God's use. The discovery of God's will for your life and the discovery of your gifts go hand in hand. Both these issues are related to the attitude of yielding to the Lordship of Christ as described in Romans 12:1, 2. When our life is available for God's use, amazing things begin to happen.

3. Concentrate on ministry to others. Spiritual gifts surface in the context of ministry and availability to others. Ask God for opportunities to minister to others. As you seek to meet needs and minister, your spiritual motivations will come to the surface and your gift will be obvious in time.

What ministries are you involved in? What opportunities could you respond to? What are ways you could be involved in ministering to others regularly?

_____

_____

---

4. Note your inclinations and your irritations. God never asks us to do any ministry without equipping us for it. The gifts are God's equipment for ministry. What are the inclinations, the interests, the abilities, the joys you find in ministry? What really fulfills you in ministry? What do you long to see happen? What burdens you? Jot down your thoughts.

Now, what are your irritations? We often tend to view people through the eyes of our gifts and ministries. What irritates you about the ministries of others? What do you wish they did differently? What needs are not being met that bother you? Write your thoughts.

---

5. Develop what you have and are using. Since spiritual gifts are to be used as instruments and not ornaments, it is obvious that their use must be cultivated. When gifts are nurtured they eventually begin to blossom. The LAMP program of lay training can help develop and hone the gifts God has given you. The purpose of each LAMP course is to provide training for, as well as in, ministry. Other LAMP books are: *Your Christian Ministry at Home, Panorama of the Bible, How to Study the Bible I and II, Welcome to Your Ministry, Welcome to the Church.* List below specific areas where you would like additional training to further enhance the gifts God has given you.

---

6. Listen to the confirmation of others. The response and feedback from the rest of the church body is a key way you can know if God is ministering through you. Think back to times others have noticed how God was using you. In what areas of ministry or relationships do you tend to get compliments?

_____

_____

7. Use your gifts in love. Some people may use their gifts to entertain others, to find status, or for personal satisfaction. But in reality, gifts can only be used effectively if they are used in love.

Study I Corinthians 13:1-3. What does Paul say here about the relationship of the gifts of the Spirit and love?

_____

Hindrances to Gift Discovery

Just as there are hindrances to physical health, so there are hindrances to spiritual health in the area of spiritual gifts and ministry. Consider these potential hindrances to gift discovery:

- Unresolved, or ongoing sins in personal living.
- Lack of involvement with the needs of others.
- Attempts to imitate the ministry or gifts of others.
- Not being open to ministries and activities that appeal to us.
- Confusion between gifts, ministries, and roles.

Take a few minutes to reflect on possible hindrances in your own life. How might you resolve these hindrances?

_____

_____

_____

_____

Conclusion

Now, are you ready? Do you have a pretty good idea of your specific gifts or gift mix? Take a few minutes to reexamine the Discovering Your Gift sections at the conclusion of the study of each gift. What would you say are your three strongest gifts? What experiences or feedback from others do you have which tend to confirm this? Be prepared to tell your group what you believe your gifts are. If you are still very unsure, review the process on the "how to" discussed in this chapter.

1. Gift: _____ Feedback: _____

_____

2. Gift: _____ Feedback: _____

_____

3. Gift: _____ Feedback: _____

_____

How to Use Your Spiritual Gifts

For many Christians in the gift discovery process, knowing where and how to enter into ministry is a frustration. In fact, that frustration keeps them from taking the all-important step of ministry commitment! This section is designed to: 1) Help you discover places your gift mix could be used. 2) Give you ideas for starting the discovery process.

Take this step seriously. It's where the rubber meets the road! Discussing gifts and understanding the importance of gifts is meaningless until you use your gifts in ministry as a servant of Jesus Christ and as a member of the Body of Christ. A good reminder is the challenging story of the talents told by Jesus in Matthew 25:14-30. As all stewards must report to the Master what they have done with what they have been given, so we will have to face Jesus and show Him how we have used the gifts He has given to us.

Instructions:

1. Check the gift or gifts you believe you have or think you may have.

2. Note possible ministries available in a local church.

3. Choose the ministry you would like to be involved in.

4. Make an appointment to talk with your pastor, elder, deacon, or ministry leader about that area of ministry and your plan to enter it.

5. Ask him or her to give you feedback about your gift and selected ministry.

6. If it appears to be definitely not the right ministry, go back to step #3 with another area of ministry.

☐ APOSTLE

Summer mission project   A new prison ministry
Short-term missions   A new ministry to any
Career missions   unreached group
Church planting

Plans for involvement: _____

_____

☐ PROPHET

Preaching   Christian action groups
Singing solos   Bible study groups
Writing   Other

Plans for involvement: _____

_____

☐ EVANGELIST

Phoning visitors
Visiting newcomers
Missions
City Gospel missions
Writing

Investigative Bible studies
Evangelistic events
One-to-one evangelism
Nursing home visitation
Other

Plans for involvement: _____

_____

☐ SHEPHERDING

Adult S.S. leader
Deacon/Deaconness
Nursing home visitation
Letter writing
Absentee follow-up
Lay counseling

Small group leader
Youth sponsor
Ushering
Shut-in visitation
Bible study group leader
Fellowship group leader
Other

Plans for involvement: _____

_____

☐ TEACHING

Sunday School teacher
Discipleship group
One-to-one discipleship
Home Bible study group
Vacation Bible School
Writing articles/books

Teacher training
Awana/Pioneers
Scouts/Brigade
Camping
Coaching
Other

Plans for involvement: _____

_____

☐ EXHORTATION

Lay counseling
Teaching Sunday School
Ministry recruiting
One-to-one discipling

Writing articles
Publicity/promotion
Music
Drama

Shepherding ministry
Youth sponsor
Telephoning

Christian action group
Coaching
Letter writing
Other

Plans for involvement: _____

_____

☐ KNOWLEDGE
Sunday School teaching
Ministry boards
Planning committees
Task forces

Seminars
Christian action group
Research writing
Library
Other

Plans for involvement: _____

_____

☐ WISDOM
Administrative boards
Leadership, oversight
Committees, task force
Nominating committee
Watch care fund
Sunday School teaching

One-to-one discipleship
Counseling
Panel discussions
Shepherding ministry
Discipleship Group
Other

Plans for involvement: _____

_____

☐ HELPS
People's needs
Facility upkeep
Clerical needs
Nursery
Food service
Receptions
Youth programs
Record keeping

Shut-in ministry
Weddings support
Bus maintenance
Sports program
Music/drama programs
Sound/lighting systems
Facility set-up
Custodial helps

Ushering   Telephoning
Funerals support   Group secretary
Tape ministry   Other

Plans for involvement: _____

_____

□ Hospitality
Home entertainment   Missions hospitality
Shepherding ministry   Ushering
Greeter   Christian action groups
Visitation   Single's ministry
Newcomer's receptions   Hosting Bible studies
Funeral receptions   Parties and socials
Wedding receptions   Other

Plans for involvement: _____

_____

□ Giving
Stewardship board   Helping the poor
Missions Support   Stewardship seminars
Ministry Support   Christian action group
Deacon fund   Other

Plans for involvement: _____

_____

□ Government
Boards/councils   Publications
Task forces   Coordinator/
Committees   superintendent
Long-range planning   Prayer chain
Tape ministry   Seminars
Sports programs   Office management
Special projects   Financial secretary
Programs involving   Other
  several people

Plans for involvement: _____

_____

□ LEADERSHIP

Board/council chairperson	Seminars
Task force chairperson	V.B.S. director
Special project leader	One-to-one discipleship
Music groups	Worship service leader
Congregation officer	Panel discussions
S. S. coordinator	Coaching
Organization president	Master of ceremonies
	Other

Plans for involvement: _____

_____

□ MERCY

Hospital visitation	Counseling
Nursing home visitation	Prayer chain
Shut-in visitation	Shepherding ministry
Ministry to the poor	Divorce recovery program
Prison ministry	Addiction programs
Big brother programs	Food closet ministry
Big sister programs	Deacon fund
Christian action programs	Other

Plans for involvement: _____

_____

□ FAITH

Leadership boards	Prayer gatherings
Planning sessions	Prayer chain
Business meetings	One-to-one discipleship
Speaking to groups	Seminars
Counseling	Fund raising
Testimonies	Writing articles
Praying for the sick	Other

Plans for involvement: _____

_____

☐ DISCERNMENT

Nominating committee
Councils/boards
Ministry recruitment
Counseling
Church business
Youth Council

Seminars/panel
   discussions
Library
One-to-one discipleship
Group participation
Bible study groups
Other

Plans for involvement: _____

_____

☐ MIRACLES

Counseling
Mission projects
Action group
Shepherding boards

Visitation/evangelism
Prayer chain
Responding to the needs
Other

Plans for involvement: _____

_____

☐ HEALING

Counseling
Visitation of sick
Prayer for the sick
Board of elders

Shepherding ministry
Mission projects
Christian action groups
Other

Plans for involvement: _____

_____

☐ TONGUES

Mission projects
Edification of the church
Cross-cultural evangelism where there is interpretation
Other

Plans for involvement: _____
_____

☐ INTERPRETATION
Only when gift of tongues is used so that others may be edified.

    The reason that nearly every category of gifts has "other" as a possibility for ministry is that there are nearly unlimited ministries for each gift. The church you are a part of may have other ministries besides the ones mentioned. Or, the Holy Spirit may be directing you to begin a new ministry or role in your church or organization. Talk to your pastor or spiritual leader(s) about it. Move ahead with faith and obedience.

    Faithfulness and obedience to the Lord in the areas of your spiritual gifts will reap tremendous rewards. It's possible that your Christian walk will be radically transformed. May God be glorified through your life as His ministry flows through you!

LESSON PLANS

Groups differ greatly in terms of how they like to structure themselves and go about the learning process. Some groups will simply want to "stick to the facts" without much personal interaction. Other groups will want to focus almost exclusively on intimate sharing and application of the lesson.

Time is also a factor. You may find that your group can function quite well by simply going over the answers to workbook questions, having prayer and a short time of fellowship. Other groups may want to spend much more time with a detailed lesson plan. So . . . consider the lesson plan activities below as *suggestions only*. Use what you can, but feel free to skip portions and/or rearrange the order to fit your group's needs.

Important Notes
- To close each Discover section (or as part of the Discuss section) of the class time: 1) Always ask for any questions/observations/sharing from the workbook assignment during the week; 2) Go over the answers to the written questions in the chapter; 3) Be sure to discuss participants' responses to the "Discovering Your Gift" inventories. Take some time to affirm those who may feel they have a particular gift (or challenge them to do some further thinking and

studying). **These three steps should be done each week—EVEN THOUGH THEY WILL NOT BE MENTIONED EACH TIME IN THE SPECIFIC LESSON PLANS BELOW.**

- Look through all of these lessons to note places where advanced preparation is needed, or materials must be gotten well before the class session. That way you won't be caught off guard.

- Try to include in all your group sessions some of the key ingredients for building group life: a time for sharing, a time for prayer, and perhaps light refreshments around which significant conversation can take place. Bible study groups can be much more than just an intellectual trip. They can become a means of developing strong bonds of Christian fellowship.

- Have an informal introductory meeting before jumping right into the study. This meeting should include: plenty of time to get acquainted with each other, time to get acquainted with the LAMP course in general, time to hand out the books and give clear instructions about what will be expected each week (but give an *ending date*, too). Be sure to start building into the group a sense of accountability for one another.

Lesson 1

FOCUS: Hand out paper and pencil and have learners write down brief descriptions of two imaginary churches: the "ideal church," and the "typical" North American church. List the characteristics, activities, climate of each.

DISCOVER: Read aloud I Cor. 12:12-27. Briefly recap the main point that we, individually, and as a church, are to carry on the ministry of Jesus in the world.

Now think back through the "perfect church" and "typical church" descriptions. List on a chalkboard or newsprint which specific features from either church could be viewed as ministries that Jesus actually did, or would *probably* do if He were physically present in the local church today. Which would he probably NOT do, or even be highly opposed to? Let students find Scripture passages in the Gospels to back up their answers.

From this exercise, lead into an "open forum" discussion. Discuss the "gap" between typical and ideal. Why is it there? What can be done to close it?

DISCUSS:
1. What are the "gaps" in our personal lives (i.e., the difference between our "ideal" functioning as Christ's minister, and the "typical" routine of our daily lives)?

2. Does Jesus really "work through" you and others in the church? What specific evidence of this have you seen in the last month or year? Share.

3. How do you envision a person who is "filled with the Spirit"? Give a practical description of how such a person might look, act, relate to others. Who have you known to be a truly Spirit-filled individual?

RESPOND: Take some time to go over answers to the last two questions in the workbook, p. 12. These questions point the direction you want learners to go in the whole course.

To close the session, recap the point made on pages 11 and 12 about God's provision: He will never give us a "Mission Impossible." Hand out 3"x5" cards and have participants write out Philippians 4:13 on one side. On the other side have them write out what seems like their own personal Mission Impossible in life right now. Give them plenty of time to think about this in silence. Then have a prayer time in which the group holds its cards up before the Lord, each person giving their "impossibilities" to God and claiming the promise of Philippians 4:13.

Lesson 2
FOCUS: Have volunteer class members "exchange" oc-

96

cupations. Give them some time to think, then let them tell (in detail, probably with some humor) what their typical day on the job is like—what they do, and how they do it. You will have a carpenter discussing his day as a lawyer; a secretary discussing her day as a zoo keeper, etc. After a few minutes, allow participants to correct the others' misconceptions about their workdays.

Then ask: "How did you feel trying to appear qualified for work you really are not too familiar with?" After some discussion, have group members share their answers to the question on page 16 about Christians being frustrated with their particular ministry.

Discover: Divide into four groups. Assign each group one of the following passages: I Cor. 12; Rom. 12; Eph. 4; I Pet. 4. Have them list all the spiritual gifts found in their particular passage, and jot down some insights about gifts that they get from the passage. Reassemble the whole group and write down the gifts in four columns (under the four Scripture passages) on a chalkboard or newsprint as group members call them out. Then discuss their insights.

Sum up this section by pointing out that: 1) Everyone has a spiritual gift; 2) gifts vary; 3) no one is qualified to do *all* ministries; 4) every gift is important.

Discuss:

1. The author writes: "There is no room for deadwood in the Body of Christ." What does this mean to you?

2. Have you ever felt exhausted spiritually or emotionally, needing the ministry of the church but feeling unable to give anything in return? How does the "deadwood" statement apply in that case? In your opinion, how does it apply in general?

3. Have you ever had the experience of being complimented for a ministry to someone (say, encouraging them) when you were not aware that you were having that effect (or even felt completely *in*effective)? Share.

Will we always be *aware* of Christ's working through us? Will we always feel energized and motivated? What is your experience?

RESPOND: Refer back to the four column listing of spiritual gifts. Ask: "What are some of your *very preliminary* observations about the areas in which you think your gift(s) might lie? What are your initial 'hunches' about your giftedness?" Ask group members to share some insights about themselves and their past experiences that give them clues as to their ministry strengths. They should focus particularly upon giving examples of times others have affirmed them about their contribution (this does NOT have to be related to any particular office or official role in the local church). Be especially careful not to "pigeonhole" anyone at this point.

Lesson 3

FOCUS: Begin by asking: "Imagine a situation in which believers were unable to speak whenever they met together. What aspects of church life would be severely limited? How would the Church be forced to change over the years? In what ways would we change the way we lived, worshiped, and ministered as Christians? What could you envision as possible *benefits* to the church in such a situation? In your opinion, would the church become more, or less effective?"

From this discussion, move to: "Let's review what we have learned about the three categories of spiritual gifts, then focus in on the two gifts of apostle and prophet."

DISCOVER: 1. In a brief lecture, go over the main points under "What Types of Gifts Are There?" 2. Ask group members to share their responses to the Scriptures they looked up under "Restricted Use" and "General Use." Summarize for them the main characteristics of the gift of apostle. 3. Ask group members to share their responses to the four questions under "The Gift of

Prophet." Summarize for them the main characteristics of the gift of prophet. 4. Now ask them to do some creative brainstorming with relation to each of these two gifts. On a chalkboard or newsprint, write their responses to: "How many different ways can you think of that these gifts could manifest themselves in Christian ministry?"

DISCUSS:
1. The gift of knowledge helps us "understand God's thoughts more deeply than would ever be possible using human reason alone." In your opinion, how does an academic discipline like Philosophy of Religion, or Philosophical Theology relate to this spiritual gift?

2. Describe a "deep" Biblical truth. To what extent is your description allowed to depart from purely Biblical language?

RESPOND: Take some time to ask: "Who thinks they may have the gift of apostle or prophet?" Have them share their insights about themselves and let the group respond with either affirmation or a challenge to do more praying and thinking about the matter. If no one in the group feels they have these gifts, make a list of those in the local church, or the Church around the world who *do*. Close in prayer for their continued ministry through God's power.

Lesson 4

FOCUS: Ask the group to write out their "first impression" answers to the following sentence starters:

• When I think of the word *evangelism* the scene that immediately pops into my mind is:

_____

• When I think of myself as a leader, I remember the time when:

_____

DISCOVER:

1. *Evangelism.* Ask someone to read Matthew 28:19, 20 aloud to the group. Point out that Christ did not command just those who were gifted evangelists to share the Gospel with the world or to teach the Bible, but He promised to be with *all of us* as we obeyed Him.

With the group pooling its Scripture knowledge, recall other Scripture passages that contain commands to Christians in general (i.e., giving, loving, hospitality, teaching, etc.). Ask: "In light of the general call to evangelize and do other Christian works, is there a difference in Christian witness between the person who feels he has the gift of evangelism and the person who doesn't? Explain your answer."

2. *Shepherding.* Use your imaginations. Visualize the following kinds of literal shepherd one at a time:

- Mr. Push the Sheep
- Mrs. Don't Bother Me
- Mr. I'll-do-it-for-you
- Mrs. Positive Encourager
- Mr. Faultfinder
- Mr. Rod-n-staff

In each of the cases above, what would a person's leadership style look like? Give specific examples of how such a person might handle problem solving in the church. What experiences have you had with these types of leaders?

DISCUSS:

1. Discuss whether pastors are the only ones with the gift to shepherd. Are they the only shepherds in the flock?

2. Shepherds guide, but the gift of shepherding is not leadership only. Discuss how a shepherd feeds and protects the sheep. In what ways might you become involved in such shepherding activities?

3. React to this statement: "Evangelism is just as much a listening task as it is a speaking task."

4. Read Eph. 4:11, 12. In what ways could you compare and contrast the shepherding gift to the work of a modern-day athletic coach?

RESPOND: Have an Open Forum discussion on this question: "How does our church's present way of approaching shepherding and evangelizing compare to the Biblical model in Ephesians 4:11, 12?" Put answers in two columns: Affirmations / Room to Improve.

To close, let participants share how they have experienced the shepherding ministry of someone else *or* how they themselves have been able to try out their shepherding abilities: helping someone trust Christ, discipling a friend, etc.

Lesson 5

FOCUS: Write the following statements on 3"x5" note cards:

1. Teachers are born, not made.
2. Teachers haven't taught until everyone has learned.
3. Those who can, do; those who can't, teach.

To introduce this lesson, give the notecards to three people in the class as they come in and ask them to be prepared to read their card aloud and tell why they agree or disagree with the statement. Give each person a minute or so to respond. Have others in the group comment and expand on what each person has said. Use these statements to stimulate learners to think about the importance of teaching.

DISCOVER:
1. *Teaching.* Go over the four points comparing the talent and gift of teaching (on page 34). Then, in order to help clarify the distinction between talent and gift, take time to focus on the author's statement: "The supernatural gift of teaching then, has the spark of God

101

to enable the effectiveness of the teacher." Ask: "Recall a time when you felt the ministry of teaching in a powerful way. You sensed the 'spark' of God moving you toward spiritual growth. What was it about the teacher/subject/environment/your personal situation that made such impact on you?" From the responses, make a list of the ways we tend to experience this "spark." Ask: "What points on this list *only apply to the gift of teaching* as used in a ministry context? What characteristics might be seen as aspects of *good teaching in general*, but which can be enhanced (by the Holy Spirit within a church context) and made effective for believers' spiritual growth?"

2. *Exhortation.* Have someone read Acts 14:21, 22. Then, on paper, have everyone finish these sentences. Share your answers to gain insight about what the gift of exhortation can bring to the Body of Christ.

• The times I am most tempted not to "remain true to the faith" are when:

• The kind of encouragement I need at those times involves:

• A time when I experienced this kind of encouragement was:

DISCUSS:
1. React: "A good teacher should be able to help people learn to think on their own—to wrestle with the issues, but not always have instant answers. That way, people grow in wisdom as well as knowledge."

2. In what ways could you envision someone abusing their supposed gift of exhortation? Have you had any experience with this?

3. Share about a time when you really benefited from another's ministry of exhortation. What took place?

RESPOND: Use the author's suggestion (on pg. 37) to close the session: Jot down the name of someone who

102

needs encouragement, and plan how to reach out to that person. Close with a period of silence as group members pray for their particular "encouragee."

Lesson 6

Focus: Refer to the opening illustration in the chapter (p. 39) about *knowing where to hit*. Ask: "In your opinion how much of what the Church does today would you describe as hit and miss? Why? What should be done?"

Discover: Let's relate these gifts to the area of outreach. Read Acts 17:16-34 aloud. Then allow a few minutes for participants to mark their Bibles at each point in the passage where they see the gift of knowledge (mark with K) or wisdom (mark with W) operating in Paul. Share insights.

Now let the group spend some time evaluating Paul's approach. If they had been Paul, how would they likely have done it differently? Come up with some practical guidelines as to how a Christian might use knowledge of the Gospel and wisdom in trying to win over the typical friendly skeptic we often meet.

Discuss:
1. The motto of a Christian college is: "All truth is God's truth." Do you agree? In what ways must we be careful about distinguishing "truth " from "spiritual truth"?

2. Some churches seem to define a person's spiritual growth in terms of Biblical knowledge alone. What other factors need to be considered when thinking about what makes a mature Christian?

Respond: Close with the leader reading aloud Paul's intercessory prayer for wisdom and knowledge as found in Ephesians 1:15-23. Have group members bow (and perhaps join hands) as they imagine the apostle speaking directly on their behalf, receiving his prayer for their own lives.

Lesson 7

FOCUS: Have group members discuss each of the three vignettes below in light of what they have learned during the week about the serving gifts. Ask: "What are the issues involved in the lives of these people? In what ways can you relate to some of their feelings? What are some indications of the presence or lack of serving gifts operating in these lives?"

• It's Sunday morning again and Mary is up early, as usual, in the church kitchen. She's hard at work, making the preparations for the morning: folding the bulletins, making Kool-Aid for Childrens' Church, coffee for the men's class. The carpet must still be swept and . . . . She's not sure she will get it all done before 9:30, but then she usually feels rushed. She pauses and thinks: "It's been six solid years like this every Sunday. How can I go on like this?"

• John feels a brief twinge of guilt as the offering plate comes his way. As the twinge passes, he puts in his regular two dollars thinking: "I certainly don't have the gift of giving, but I guess that's good—otherwise I'd never be able to save enough for a housing down payment for my family."

• Sue is in a real panic. The guests will be here any minute, and the house just isn't spic and span the way she always tries to keep it. She says to herself as the doorbell rings: "I'll think of some excuse. Besides, those kids of theirs will probably get fingerprints all over everything anyway. Why can't they control them better?"

DISCOVER: Divide into three groups and assign each group one of these passages: Helps, Acts 9:36-39; Hospitality, Genesis 18:1-8; Giving, II Cor. 9:6-15. Each group is a ministerial meeting. The pastors are working together on a sermon outline for the passage. Each sermon should have the following elements:

Title:
Theme:
Key Biblical Truth:
Introduction:
Three points:
Application point:
Concluding Illustration:

(You may want to have sheets of paper with these headings to hand out to each group member for filling in their ideas.) When the "sermons" are completed have the group choose one of the "pastors" to share their groups' sermon outline.

DISCUSS: In your opinion, how important—for deciding whether you have one of the serving gifts described in the chapter—is the criterion of being able to serve *with joy*? That is, if you feel a need to help others but find that you are rarely doing it with a sense of joy and fulfillment, do you think you have this spiritual gift of helps? What may be the problem? Where does the idea of "sacrificial" service fit in?

RESPOND: Close with prayer and these suggestions for a practical response:

1. This week (or for the next couple of weeks) give at least one secret gift each week.

2. Invite someone to share a meal, dessert, or your home for an evening.

3. Try to find at least one area where you can be helpful. (It doesn't have to be a big job.)

Encourage learners to share their results—not just what they gave—but how they felt, how they were received, etc.

Lesson 8

FOCUS: Begin by handing each person large triangles (cut out of construction paper, with about 8" sides). Have them label these to show a flowchart of their company or department at work. (Or, for those not working: a group or organization they are involved with, etc.) They should make clear which point of the triangle is the "top." When they are finished, let a few volunteer to explain how their company is structured, and go into a little detail (perhaps with examples) about the basic management style or attitude of their supervisors or leaders.

DISCOVER: Now have everyone read Mark 10:42-44 (see also Jn. 13:1-17) silently. Hand out a second set of triangles (different color). Have participants label them to show Jesus' basic teaching on leadership attitudes. Where is the "top" on this triangle?

Ask: "In your opinion, how practical is Jesus' servanthood model of leadership? In what ways is our church, within the form of government already set up, actually applying the attitude Jesus speaks of in this passage?" "In what areas might we be able to improve? How could such change *begin?*" List suggestions on a chalkboard or newsprint.

DISCUSS:
1. Modern management theory stresses the concept of "ownership." That is, the more a group has a say in formulating its own directions, goals, procedures, the more committed it will be to accomplishing those goals. Do you agree? Can this principle be applied to a church governing board? How?

2. For anyone in a church leadership role, where would you draw the line between "sacrificial servanthood" and being a "doormat" (being at the whim and mercy of everyone at all times)? Try to use a hypothetical case in your answer.

RESPOND: For this session, use the response time to do a GROUP CHECK. Look at the dynamics of what's happening in the group now and over the last few weeks. How are people feeling about the course so far? About their relationships with one another? About the structure of the class time? Other concerns? Allow plenty of time for response and honest consideration of suggestions for solving any problems that might be raised. Every group needs to check its pulse from time to time. Here's your chance.

Also, check on their progress in gift discovery. How are they doing? Encourage them not to be discouraged if they don't know what their gift is yet, but to keep trying out new opportunities to explore their gifts. Those who think they've found their gifts may be eager to tell what they've learned and how they plan to (or do) use their gifts. The "bottom line" of this course is *using* what has been learned. Gifts may be embryonic— too small yet to be sure of. But, as learners see that it's "warmer" over here and "colder" over there—their understanding will grow.

Lesson 9

Focus: Begin by asking the group to react to the ministry of Mother Theresa as described in the chapter opening. While not everyone can be like her, each Christian is commanded to show love for others. Ask: "How can a person with the gift of showing mercy maintain an attitude of cheerfulness?" Provide an opportunity at this time for learners to talk about acts of mercy that they have done, received, or seen in the past.

Discover: Let's spend some time looking more closely at each of the gifts described in this chapter. Divide into three groups.

1. *Mercy.* This group will read Luke 10:25-37. Have them work together to develop a modern-day Good Samaritan story that depicts a practical opportunity for showing mercy in the course of our everyday lives. Share with the group, asking them to suggest ways that it is realistic, or could be made more so, in light of their own experience.

2. *Faith.* This group will read Mark 11:22-26. In light of Jesus' call for a mountain-moving faith, they will formulate a list of "faith busters." These would be attitudes and actions that we typically find hindering our increase in faith, or tempting us to fall back on our own resources. Share with the group, asking them to add their own ideas to the list. Then discuss possible ways to start overcoming some of these faith busters.

3. *Discernment.* This group will study the five passages on page 63. They will try to come up with modern-day examples of issues in the Church at large about which Christians need to exercise discernment. Share with the group, asking for additional ideas, then discuss practical ways to avoid the pitfalls.

DISCUSS:
1. Who do you know that has the gift of showing mercy? Faith? Discernment? What is the evidence you have seen in them (or yourself?) and their ministries?

2. Do you feel there is a lack of the mountain-moving kind of faith Jesus spoke of? Why?

3. Give some examples of proper and improper ways a person might go about exercising the gift of discernment.

RESPOND: Close with a time of conversational prayer for renewed faith, concentrating particularly upon the individual concerns raised in the discussion about "faith busters."

Lesson 10

FOCUS: Present the following mini case study. Then let participants take turns being the pastor, explaining how they would deal with the situation:

Karen, a 20-year-old college student and brand-new Christian, has just landed in the hospital with a diagnosis of cancer. The night before she had been to a dancing and drinking party with some of her non-Christian friends—hoping for an opportunity to tell them about her newfound faith. She had looked forward to learning more about the Christian life, but now all her plans for the future seem so bleak. . . . Her mother and father have tried to comfort her but they seem to be overcome with grief and anger, afraid to listen to Karen's deepest fears and seemingly unanswerable questions. She called for the pastor of her new church.

"Pastor, why did this happen to me? Should I have stayed home from that party? You know about God and the Bible. Please give me some *answers*! Can't God *do* something? What about healing?"

As pastor, you feel a need to do some explaining. You think for a moment, open your Bible, then look up at Karen and begin: "Karen, it's like this . . . .

DISCOVER: Write each of the following references on a slip of paper and pass out the slips: Exodus 15:25; Joshua 10:12; I Kings 18:38; II Kings 20:11; John 9:7; Acts 3:7; Acts 28:5; Acts 6:8 and Acts 28:8. Ask participants to read the verse aloud and explain what sign gift was in action here and what its purpose was. When all have shared, summarize this exercise by reminding the group that miracles and healings were always done to reveal God more clearly. Some signs demonstrated God's power; others, His loving-kindness for His people; still other signs authenticated His messengers.

DISCUSS:
1. Will a person who has witnessed a divine miracle *always* come to faith in Christ? Why?

2. In what ways can you envision the gifts of miracles and healing being abused? Do you have any specific examples?

3. Describe how your own church interprets and puts into practice the instructions for dealing with the sick in James 5:13-26. How do these instructions relate to the gift of healing?

RESPOND: This might be a good place to spend some time in prayer for the sick. Make a list of those in your church or community who need prayer for encouragement and healing. Let each group member take a name and pray for that person individually.

Lesson 11

FOCUS: Begin with this question: "Who has a story to tell about a time when they tried to communicate with a person of another language? What happened?"

DISCOVER: Ask someone to read Acts 2:1-4 aloud. Take a few minutes to discuss what actually took place that day. With the help of the group, develop a definition for the gift of speaking in tongues.

This gift was used as a sign for unbelievers. Have learners share the purpose of the apostles speaking in tongues in Acts 2:1-13; to the Gentiles at Caesarea (in Acts 10:44-48); and the Ephesians in Acts 19:1-7. Ask: "From these episodes can we conclude that God intended the gift of tongues to evangelize others?" Discuss:

This gift is clearly restricted in Scripture. Discuss the problems the Corinthians faced and the guidelines for speaking in tongues recorded in I Cor. 14.

Be sure that you leave the group with a positive attitude toward those who may hold a different opinion toward speaking in tongues than they do.

DISCUSS:

1. To what degree is the difference of opinion among Christians (about the appropriateness of tongues for today) a matter of preference for a particular style of worship? Or the degree of comfort a person may have with displaying emotion in worship?

2. How might the gifts of tongues and interpretation relate to a person's special capacity to work with languages (eg., in a ministry of Bible translation, such as Wycliffe Translators)?

Respond: Close with conversational prayer that focuses on the cross-cultural missions work of your local church or denomination.

Lesson 12

Focus: Have students react to the Yates' Pool story with the following sharing exercise. Hand each a sheet of paper with this typed on it:

When I think about my life and my own "spiritual gift net worth" the words that come to mind are:

Only my accountant knows for sure
Buried Treasures
What a spendthrift!
Dirt poor
Yipee! Just struck it rich!
Looking for a good investment
Considering a sellout
Yuppie
Living on a real tight budget

Let students share what they meant by their answers, giving other group members insight into how this study has affected their attitudes and plans for future ministry.

Discover: Now let's look more closely at a Bible passage that has crucial significance for the way we view our gifts and their use. Prepare a brief lecture on "The Love Chapter," I Corinthians 13. Make sure you cover the following points:

1. Love is the bottom line in all ministry relationships.

2. One's gifts and abilities may be powerful—even miraculous—but ineffective when exercised with the wrong motive or attitude.

3. Reemphasize the author's statement: "When you genuinely love others and seek to serve them in love, the gifts you have will surface and their effectiveness will come to the forefront!"

Now take some time to go over the participants' answers to the questions under "How to Discover Your Gifts." and "Hindrances to Gift Discovery." From there, go on to the discussion questions below or move directly to the response section.

DISCUSS: Because this is the last session, it is very important to facilitate good, meaningful closure. Perhaps a good way would be to spend quite a bit of time simply sharing responses to the group's answers under "Conclusion" and their thinking about future ministry in light of the options they may have checked on pp. 87-93.

RESPOND: Make sure there is plenty of time for mutual affirmation and encouragement before the session ends. You might want to lay plans for the group to meet again in a couple of months for a time of fellowship. Or, plan a potluck dinner in the near future as a means of celebrating your time together.

Close the session with a circular group conversational prayer (perhaps holding hands) in which each person thanks God for the person on his or her immediate right—thanking God for who that person is, affirming their desire to do God's will, and lifting before God their special needs and concerns.